McGrew and Fenlon

Table of Contents

Table of Contents

Introduction

The DNA leans this way

McGrew/MacGrew

James C. McGrew, born in Pennsylvania, in 1761 (later lived in Kingwood, VA) was one of the first known McGrew historians, and he wrote 'There is no doubt that the McGrews who migrated from Ireland to America were native Scots or descendants of Scotch immigrants who left Scotland to avoid religious persecution. (this was found in 'History of the McGrew family' prepared for a McGrew reunion that was held at Olympia Park near McKeesport, PA on August 15, 1912). James C. McGrew also stated that his grandfather (Robert McGrew) came to America from Omagh, County Tyrone, Ireland wearing a blue scotch bonnet.

According to the Coat of Arms & Family Crests book by Berke's   now shortened to Grewer and Grewar is found principally in the south of Perthshire, about Glenartney, and it was common in Dunblane and Doune in the 17th and 18th centuries. The family of the North as a sept are merged mostly in the Frasers and adjoining clans. Other spellings of the name include MacGRUER, MacGROUGHTER, MacGROWTHER, MacCRITER and McHRUDDER. The earliest recorded of the name is Gilawnane McCrouder, who was witness to a charter in 1447, and Gilbert McGrevar was a tenant of Dowart, Stragarta in 1499. The use of fixed surnames or descriptive names appears to have commenced in France about the year 1000, and such names were introduced into Scotland through the Normans a little over one hundred years later, although the custom of using them was by no means common for many years afterwards. During the reign of Malcolm Ceannmor (1057-1093) the latter directed his chief subjects, after the custom of other nations, to adopt surnames from their territorial possessions, and there created 'The first erlis that euir was in Scotland'. Duncan M'Rudder was a witness in Perth in 1547, and Alexander M'Gruder held the parsonage of Lochals in 1550. John McGrader (arrow-maker) in Blainrowar was fined in 1613 for reset (receiver or concealer of stolen goods) of Clan Gregor.

Family stories gives this

The McGrew info is interesting. The MacGregor clan originally had lands near the head of Loch Awe, near Glen Strae and Glen Orchy. This is in Argyll and Bute, near the area called Lorn, in west central Scotland. They later moved to the northern Loch Lomond area mainly due to clan feuds, especially with the large Campbell clan in Argyll. Most of their lands were in and around what was once called the Flanders Moss (since drained), Loch Lomond, the Trossachs, Glen Gyle, and Glen Douchart. They used this for their "protection" service - they tended to have a fair share of cattle rievers it seems. The name was proscribed after a tiff in 1603 called the Slaughter of Lennox, where many Buchannons were killed and then 200 Colquhouns were killed at the Battle of Glen Fruin. Archibald Campbell, 7th Earl of Campbell used his connections with King James to get this done.

Around this time, King James opened up lands in Ulster (Northern Ireland) and many Scots, especially Catholics, moved there - over 250,000 families is what is have read at the Ulster-American Folk Center in Armagh, N. Ireland. Most of these Scots came to America - these are the TRUE Scots-Irish.

There does not seem to be any Clan MacGregor offshoots in Anstruther, Fife. It would be very surprising if McGrew descendants came from there. Some possibly moved there, but in the early 1600's, people tended to not move much in Scotland. Robert Roy MacGregor - "Rob Roy" - actually went by Robert Roy Campbell (his mother was a Campbell). No one using the name MacGregor could legally transact any business and could be killed without penalty! Rob Roy's grave is in Balquhidder, Scotland, just north of Calendar in the Trossachs, where most MacGregor's remained.

The McGrew family was an off-shoot of the Clan MacGregor which was a distinct clan in the Scottish Highlands as early as 1296. The family McGrew moved from Scotland to Ireland when they refused to fight and they were ordered to take another name. Most settled in County Tyrone. The listings of the families in the clan include the name McGrewer which was shortened to McGrew when the families moved to Ireland. "The MacGregors were a hardy lot and resented having their lands taken by the King, and when they rose in rebellion he ordered the clan disbanded and banished and the name not to be spoken in Scotland again. This went on for some time, and eventually some lands were restored, but in the meantime many had been driven out and the clan scattered.

The clan is of royal descent. The genealogy in the DEAN'S BOOK by Duncan is stated to have been written in 1512, and to have been taken "from the books of the genealogies of the kings." It traces the descent through Hugh of Urchy, from Alpin, who ruled about 787, the father of Kenneth, 'High King of Scotland. The suppression of the name was annulled by Parliament in 1774, but that of course, was after the McGREWs were settled in America. At the time of the suppression of the clan many young children were taken to Ireland and also at about that time England sent many of the hardy Scots to Ireland to control the Irish. The Scots were not happy in Ireland and after a generation or two emigrated to America, where, under Penn's rules, they could have freedom of religion. In the family records, we know that Robert McGrew and wife Isabella came from County Tyrone, Ireland 1726/7 and that when Robert arrived he was wearing a blue Scotch bonnet or Glengary cap."

The family was originally from Scots Highlands near Anstruther, County Fife on the Firth of Forth, 15 miles Southeast of Cupar, according to Thomas Dixon Graham. Legend says that King Edward banished MacGregors because he believed they were "too patriotic for the safety of his throne."

Fenlon

Fenlon Family History
Fenlon Name Meaning
Irish: reduced Anglicized form of Gaelic Ó Fionnaláin 'descendant of Fionnalán', a personal name from a diminutive of fionn 'fair', 'white' (see Finn 1). English (Huguenot): altered form of French Fénelon (see Fenelon).

Source: Dictionary of American Family Names ©2013, Oxford University Press

Recorded in the spellings of Fenlin, Fenelon, Fenlon, Finl;and and possibly others, this is an ancient Irish and sometimes a French surname. It derives from the pre 10th century Gaelic O'Fionnallain, which translates literally as the descendant of the son of the fair one, and is probably a reference to the first chieftain, who may have been a Viking. The Norsemen conquered much of Ireland in the 8th century a.d., and Dublin was their capital. The name would seem to be a reference to one who was fair haired and fair skin, whilst the original natives like the Welsh and Olde English were more swarthy and dark complexioned. Certainly the vast majority of Irish surnames are nicknames from the original chiefs, and this name is no exception. It is not clear when the O' prefix was lost but it was probably in the 17th century when name spellings took on a more English form. The clan originated in County Westmeath, and were also "fused" with French Fenelons, who were Huguenots who entered both England and Ireland as refugees in the 18th century.

Benjamin Gilbert McGrew
Katherine Sowash Howell
Rev. Loren B Leasure
Anna Overholt Tintsman
Edward Fenlon
Mary Murphy
John C. Hintz
Emile W. Kroplien
Archibald Benjamin McGrew Sr.
Minnie E. Leasure
Joseph Patrick Fenlon
Emily Hintz
Albert Douthett McGrew
Bertha Marie Fenlon
Mary Fenlon McGrew

Ancestors of Mary Fenlon McGrew

First Generation

1. Mary Fenlon McGrew, daughter of **Albert Douthett McGrew** and **Bertha Marie Fenlon,** was born on 18 Sep 1934 in Franklin, Venango County, Pennsylvania.

Mary married **Charles Gorham "Chuck" Brewer** on 14 Jan 1958 in Franklin, Venango County, Pennsylvania.

Second Generation (Parents)

2. Albert Douthett McGrew, son of **Archibald Benjamin McGrew Sr.** and **Minnie E. Leasure,** was born on 22 Jan 1898 in Greensburg, Westmoreland County, Pennsylvania, died on 13 Jul 1998 in Kerr County, Texas at age 100, and was buried in Fenlons Cemetery Mackinac County, Michigan.

Albert married **Bertha Marie Fenlon** on 14 Feb 1924 in Wayne, Mackinac, Michigan.

Children from this marriage were:

    i.   **Anne Leasure McGrew** was born on 2 Jan 1926 in Pittsburgh, Allegheny County, Pennsylvania, died on 25 Dec 2011 in Walnut Creek, Contra Costa County, California at age 85, and was buried in Fenlons Cemetery.

    ii.   **Natalie Jane McGrew** was born on 20 Aug 1929 in Pittsburgh, Allegheny County, Pennsylvania.

1   iii.   **Mary Fenlon McGrew**

Ancestors of Mary Fenlon McGrew

3. Bertha Marie Fenlon, daughter of **Joseph Patrick Fenlon** and **Emily Hintz,** was born on 9 Jun 1898 in Hessel, Mackinac County, Michigan, died on 7 Apr 1993 in Alpine, Brewster, Texas at age 94, and was buried in Fenlons Cemetery Mackinac County, Michigan.

Bertha married **Albert Douthett McGrew** on 14 Feb 1924 in Wayne, Mackinac, Michigan.

Third Generation (Grandparents)

4. Archibald Benjamin McGrew Sr., son of **Benjamin Gilbert McGrew** and **Katherine Sowash "Kate" Howell,** was born on 29 Mar 1861 in Westmoreland County, Pennsylvania, died on 14 Apr 1919 in Greensburg, Westmoreland County, Pennsylvania at age 58, and was buried in Saint Clair Cemetery.

Archibald married **Minnie E. Leasure** on 23 Oct 1883 in Greensburg, Westmoreland County, Pennsylvania.

Children from this marriage were:

- i. **Lillian E. McGrew** was born on 16 May 1885 in Greensburg, Westmoreland County, Pennsylvania, died in 1940 in Greensburg, Westmoreland County, Pennsylvania at age 55, and was buried in Saint Clair Cemetery.
- ii. **Roy Leasure McGrew** was born on 11 Feb 1888 in Greensburg, Westmoreland County, Pennsylvania, died on 28 May 1960 in Pittsburgh, Allegheny County, Pennsylvania at age 72, and was buried in Homewood Cemetery.
- iii. **May Tintsman McGrew** was born on 15 Apr 1890 in Westmoreland County, Pennsylvania, died in 1986 at age 96, and was buried in Saint Clair Cemetery.
- iv. **Archibald Benjamin McGrew Jr** was born on 2 Feb 1893 in Greensburg, Westmoreland County, Pennsylvania, died on 6 Dec 1973 in Indiana, Indiana County, Pennsylvania at age 80, and was buried in Oakland Cemetery and Mausoleum.
- v. **Minnie Emma McGrew** was born on 20 Jul 1895 in Greensburg, Westmoreland County, Pennsylvania, died on 13 Oct 1982 in Pittsburgh, Allegheny County, Pennsylvania at age 87, and was buried in Homewood Cemetery.
- 2 vi. **Albert Douthett McGrew**
- vii. **Helen Overholt McGrew** was born on 6 Oct 1901 in Westmoreland County, Pennsylvania, died in 1981 at age 80, and was buried in Saint Clair Cemetery.

Produced by: Tennessee Research Company on 5 Sep 2019

5. Minnie E. Leasure, daughter of **Rev. Loren Bigelow Leasure** and **Anna Overholt Tintsman,** was born on 21 Jan 1864 in Westmoreland County, Pennsylvania, died on 28 Jun 1952 in Westmoreland County, Pennsylvania at age 88, and was buried in Saint Clair Cemetery.

Minnie married **Archibald Benjamin McGrew Sr.** on 23 Oct 1883 in Greensburg, Westmoreland County, Pennsylvania.

6. Joseph Patrick Fenlon, son of **Edward Fenlon** and **Mary Murphy,** was born on 17 Mar 1866 in Bagenalstown, County Carlow, Ireland, died on 18 Jan 1941 in Sault Sainte Marie, Chippewa County, Michigan at age 74, and was buried in Fenlons Cemetery.

Research Notes: THE JOSEPH FENLON FAMILY Bertha Fenlon McGrew Joseph Patrick Fenlon, a pioneer and resident of Mackinac County for 55 years, came from Ireland to Canada at the age of 16 together with his parents, seven brothers, and two sisters in 1882. They first settled in Seaforth, Ontario (north and slightly west of London), where they remained for 3 years. In 1885 Joseph and apparently brothers John and Edward migrated north to Sault Ste. Marie(probably via the Canadian Pacific steamer out of Owen Sound) and thence entered the US. It is said that at first they worked the lumber camps, probably the ones operated by Smith & Hossack near Rader and the Gogomain, whence Joseph walked, following lumber company tote roads and then the Indian trail that came out near the center of what now is Hessel, at the marina. The first sight that met his eyes was that of two Indian squaws in birch bark canoes lifting nets, which were filled with jumbo whitefish of a size no longer caught. The beauties and possibilities of the location so impressed him that, there and then he decided to settle near the spot. He must have returned to the Gogomain to lumber through the winter and then come back, with his brothers, in the spring. For in April of 1886 John and Edward filed side- by-side homesteads behind the Wendell owned shorefront and immediately north of those filed the previous year by Frank Pillman and David Stuart. Joseph filed for his in September north and slightly west of Mackinac Bay, behind the Wendells and George Andrews. Joseph first clerked for the Hessel family in their store, but in 1891 he and his younger brother James, it seems that by now the rest of the family had arrived, built a general store on the Hessel site of what is now the James Bowlby residence. Hessel Restaurant. This was a very traditional country store, though it later became principally a market, dealing in green groceries, produce, meat, and general merchandise, from basic hardware's, to fabrics to toys. This burned and rebuilt in 1908, operated as The Fenlon Brothers Stores until 1950, when it was first leased, then sold to Forrest B. Dick Church of Cedarville by Hintz Fenlon, Josephs son and heir to the store. Besides Hintz, Joseph had two daughter, Ellen (Mrs. Paul Tobin) later of Akron Ohio and Bertha (Mrs. Albert D. McGrew) of Franklin, Pennsylvania. (This is who Longs bought it from in October 1986) Unable to obtain land in Ireland as a Roman Catholic under English Protestant rule, Joseph was obsessed with the acquisition of property-as his means would permit. He thus often attended and invested at tax sales. As land was acquired with suitable timber on it, the Fenlon brothers engaged in the lumber business together with their retail trade enterprise, the one business complementing the other. James died at the age of 35 and was buried on the homestead where his parents could see his grave from the window of their home. Many of the Fenlon descendants are now buried there. The township eventually took over the burial ground, but it is

still the Fenlon Cemetery. Joseph died in 1940 at age 74. Both Joseph and his son, Hintz, became fluent in the Chippewa language so that they could easily communicate with the local Indians, of whom there were a goodly number through the early days of this century. In 1907 or 08 Joseph, Hintz and Bertha were inducted into the local Chippwea band with appropriate ceremonies. A great feast was held at Chief Sabtigos home, the war dance was danced, and then the pipe of peace was smoked by all. The pipe was a beautiful article, its stem was covered with Indian symbols and the bowl was of red clay inclaid with pewter. Joseph was declared Chief of the White Men and given the name Ossowanimikee, which means Yellow Thunder. Hintz was Wasagesic and Bertha, Wasagesic go quay. Bertha now of McAllen Texas still used the old family home as a summer residence. The house was built in 1897 by Joseph Kramen, boat builder and part time carpenter, without benefit of either plumb bob or square.
Written by Albert D. McGrew

Joseph married **Emily Hintz** on 25 Mar 1895 in St Ignace, MacKinac County, Michigan.

Children from this marriage were:

	i.	**Ellen Louise Fenlon** was born on 31 Jan 1896 in Mackinac County, Michigan.
	ii.	**Hintz Joseph Fenlon** was born on 15 Feb 1897 in Mackinac County, Michigan, died on 21 Sep 1950 in Mackinac County, Michigan at age 53, and was buried in Fenlons Cemetery.
3	iii.	**Bertha Marie Fenlon**

7. Emily Hintz, daughter of **John C. Hintz** and **Emilie W. Kroplien,** was born on 7 May 1871 in Mackinac County, Michigan, died on 5 Oct 1934 in Mackinac County, Michigan at age 63, and was buried in Fenlons Cemetery.

Emily married **Joseph Patrick Fenlon** on 25 Mar 1895 in St Ignace, MacKinac County, Michigan.

Fourth Generation (Great-Grandparents)

8. Benjamin Gilbert McGrew, son of **Archibald Blackburn McGrew** and **Susannah Gilbert,** was born on 31 Mar 1834 in Westmoreland County, Pennsylvania, died on 3 Aug 1904 in Allegheny County, Pennsylvania at age 70, and was buried in Saint Clair Cemetery.

Benjamin married **Katherine Sowash "Kate" Howell** on 17 Nov 1857 in Turtle Creek, Allegheny County, Pennsylvania.

Children from this marriage were:

	i.	**Minerva Etta McGrew** was born on 9 Sep 1858 and died on 9 Dec 1927 at age 69.
	ii.	**John Franklin McGrew** was born in 1859, died on 20 May 1910 at age 51, and was buried in Saint Clair Cemetery.
4	iii.	**Archibald Benjamin McGrew Sr.**
	iv.	**Dilwyn Gilbert McGrew** was born on 14 Sep 1864, died on 15 Nov 1923 at age 59, and was buried in Saint Clair Cemetery.
	v.	**William Edgar McGrew** was born in 1866 and died on 15 Jan 1913 at

Benjamin Gilbert McGrew

age 47.

vi. **Sarah Shirwell McGrew** was born on 29 Dec 1867 and died on 25 Dec 1951 at age 83.

vii. **Susan Belle McGrew** was born on 7 Mar 1870 and died on 14 Apr 1937 at age 67.

viii. **Wesley Cope McGrew** was born on 24 Mar 1875 and died on 15 Mar 1946 at age 70.

9. Katherine Sowash "Kate" Howell, daughter of **John Arnold Howell** and **Sarah Sowash,** was born on 31 Mar 1839 in Allegheny County, Pennsylvania, died on 8 Jan 1910 in Pittsburgh, Allegheny County, Pennsylvania at age 70, and was buried in Saint Clair Cemetery.

Katherine married **Benjamin Gilbert McGrew** on 17 Nov 1857 in Turtle Creek, Allegheny County, Pennsylvania.

10. Rev. Loren Bigelow Leasure, son of **Abraham Leasure** and **Barbara Anna Lobingier,** was born on 26 Oct 1826 in Madison, Westmoreland County, Pennsylvania, died on 9 Nov 1881 in Greensburg, Westmoreland County, Pennsylvania at age 55, and was buried in Saint Clair Cemetery.

Loren married **Anna Overholt Tintsman** on 26 Nov 1855.

Children from this marriage were:

i. **Mariah Elizabeth Leasure** was born on 20 Oct 1857 in Irwin, Westmoreland County, Pennsylvania, died on 8 Aug 1938 in Jeannette, Westmoreland County, Pennsylvania at age 80, and was buried in Brush Creek Cemetery.

ii. **Israel Painter Leasure** was born on 11 Oct 1859 in Hempfield Township, Westmoreland County, Pennsylvania,, died on 21 Jan 1939 in Greensburg, Westmoreland County, Pennsylvania at age 79, and was buried in Union Cemetery.

iii. **Ida Leasure** was born on 24 Nov 1861 in Greensburg, Westmoreland County, Pennsylvania, died on 7 Feb 1946 in Greensburg, Westmoreland County, Pennsylvania at age 84, and was buried in Saint Clair Cemetery.

5   iv. **Minnie E. Leasure**

v. **Anna O. Leasure** was born in 1866 in Greensburg, Westmoreland County, Pennsylvania, died in 1885 in Greensburg, Westmoreland County, Pennsylvania at age 19, and was buried in Saint Clair Cemetery.

vi. **Loran Bigelow Leasure Jr** was born in 1870 in Greensburg, Westmoreland County, Pennsylvania, died in 1957 in Greensburg, Westmoreland County, Pennsylvania at age 87, and was buried in Saint Clair Cemetery.

vii. **Edna Leasure** was born in 1874 in Greensburg, Westmoreland County, Pennsylvania, died in 1971 in Greensburg, Westmoreland County, Pennsylvania at age 97, and was buried in Saint Clair Cemetery.

viii. **John F. Leasure** was born on 13 Jun 1877 in Greensburg, Westmoreland County, Pennsylvania, died in Aug 1965 in Greensburg, Westmoreland County, Pennsylvania at age 88, and was buried in Saint Clair Cemetery.

11. Anna Overholt Tintsman, daughter of **John Tintsman** and **Anna Stauffer Overholt,** was born on 29 Dec 1838 in Westmoreland County, Pennsylvania, died on 31 Jul 1941 in Greensburg, Westmoreland County, Pennsylvania at age 102, and was buried in Saint Clair Cemetery.

Research Notes: GREENSBURG'S OLDEST WOMAN IS DEAD AT AGE OF 102

GREENSBURG, July 31. - UP - The city's oldest woman, Mrs. Anna T. Leasure, 102, died today. She was the widow of the Rev. Loren Bigelow Leasure, a Reformed Church preacher, who held pastorates in Somerset County, Kittanning, Wilkinsburg, Emlenton and Scottsdale, Pa., prior to his death in 1881. Mrs. Leasure, who would have been 103 years old in December, is survived by five children, including Mrs. A. D. McGrew, Pittsburgh.

From: The News-Herald, Franklin, Pennsylvania, on Thursday July 31, 1941, Page 14

LEASURE FUNERAL SATURDAY

Funeral services for Greensburg's oldest resident, Mrs. Anna Tinstman Leasure who died at her home in Harrison avenue at 10 o'clock Thursday morning, will be held there at 8 o'clock Saturday afternoon. Rev. Paul Reid Pontius, D. D. minster of the Second Evangelical and Reformed Church of this city, will be in charge of the services which

Anna Overholt Tintsman

will be private as will the interment following in the St. Clair cemetery. Friends are asked to omit flowers.

From: The Greenburg Daily Tribune, Greensburg, Pennsylvania, on Friday August 1, 1941, Page 10

Correction Maiden Name: Tintsman

MRS. LEASURE CELEBRATES ROUND CENTURY OF LIVING

by Lewis C. Walkinshaw

It will come to an extremely small number of us to reach the age of 100 years, but such was the accomplishment of Mrs. Anna Tintsman Leasure of Harrison Avenue, Greensburg. Her home was the Mecca for a host of admiring friends, relatives and descendants. Mrs. Leasure is a descendant of Abraham Overholt, who was born in Bucks County, PA, in 1774 and came to East Huntingdon Township at the present West Overton in 1800. Their daughter, Anna Overholt, born July 4, 1812, married John Tintsman in 1830 who died in 1866. To this marriage were born Maria, Jacob O., Abraham O., Henry O., Anna, widow of Rev. L. B. Leasure, John O. who died in the Civil War, Elizabeth, Emma, wife of D. W. J. K. Kline and Christian S. O. Tintsman. Jacob Tintsman was born in Bucks County, January 13, 1773, married in Chester County December 11, 1708 to Anna Fox who was born in Chester County August 8, 1779. Ten children were born to this marriage, and among them John Tintsman, born January 29, 1807, in East Huntingdon Township where he lived as a respected farmer. Anna Fox Tintsman died in 1877.

The husband of the centenarian, Rev. Loren Bigelow Leasure, was a son of Abraham and Barbara (Lobingier) Leasure and was born near Madison on October 26, 1828. He was married to Anna Tintsman November 26, 1855 and became the father of eight children. He was licensed to preach by the quarterly conference of the United Brethren Church on January 30, 1852 and was ordained by the annual conference at Liverpool, Perry County January 4, 1862. He changed his denominational affiliations and was received into the Westmoreland Classes of the Reformed Church in 1868, serving pastorates in Somerset County, Kittanning, Emlenton, Wilkinsburg and Scottdale. He died November 9, 1881 at the age of 55 years.

Mrs. Leasure's late husband came of the distinctive pioneer stock of Phillip Heck, a member of Captain Casper Walthour's Company in the Fort Walthour settlement. One of Phillip Heck's daughters married Walthour, another Fisher, a third Garvin and a fourth Leasure. So that, good neighbor and friend, has brought into her life the stability of pioneer Americanism, good health and a sunny disposition.

It was a great pleasure to have her break a rule of 25 or more years' standing--not to have her picture taken and to gracefully pose for a characteristic likeness yesterday. In doing this she accredited to the desire of her many friends and children. In the course of the conversation, the Battle of Gettysburg was referred to. We told her how the late Hugh W. Walkinshaw, then a lad of 13 years at Saltsburg and the late Isaac Sherrick, picking wheat sheaves in his uncle's (Peter Sherrick) wheat field near West Overton, both declared that they hear the cannonading at Gettysburg on that eventful July day in 1863. Mrs. Leasure quickly retorted that she heard it, too. Her memory was keen enough to recall many other incidents through the years.

All honor to Greensburg's lovely lady, who has now entered the second century of a busy and happy life. Her friends and family heaped upon her many birthday cards, bouquets of beautiful flowers and other gifts and thus helped her to enjoy one of the happiest days of her life, as she was glad to express it.

Anna married **Rev. Loren Bigelow Leasure** on 26 Nov 1855.

12. Edward Fenlon, son of **John Fenlon** and **Ellen Scott,** was born on 30 Apr 1826 in Bagenalstown, County Carlow, Ireland, was christened in May 1826, died on 8 Feb 1920 in Mackinac County, Michigan at age 93, and was buried in Fenlons Cemetery.

Research Notes: Immigration Year   1886

Edward married **Mary Murphy** in 1855 in County Carlow, Ireland.

Children from this marriage were:

	i.	**John Fenlon** was born in 1856 in County Carlow, Ireland and died on 21 Jun 1941 in St Ignace, MacKinac County, Michigan at age 85.
6	ii.	**Joseph Patrick Fenlon**
	iii.	**Edward Paul Fenlon** was born on 13 Jul 1870 in Bagenalstown, County Carlow, Ireland, died on 19 Jul 1943 in Mackinac County, Michigan at age 73, and was buried in Fenlons Cemetery.
	iv.	**Thomas Fenlon** was born on 23 Aug 1870 in Kilcock, County Kildare, Ireland and died between Apr and Jun 1939 in County Carlow, Ireland.

    v.   **Ellen Fenlon** was born in 1872 in County Carlow, Ireland and died in 1902 in Mackinac County, Michigan at age 30.

    vi.   **William A. Fenlon** was born in May 1873 in Ireland, died on 23 Jun 1946 in Everett, Snohomish County, Washington at age 73, and was buried in Evergreen Cemetery.

    vii.   **Bridget Fenlon** was born in 1874 in County Carlow, Ireland and died in 1883 at age 9.

    viii.   **James Fenlon** was born on 20 Oct 1874 in Godgestown, Kildare, Ireland, died in 1910 in St Ignace, MacKinac County, Michigan at age 36, and was buried in Fenlons Cemetery.

    ix.   **Michael Frances Fenlon** was born on 10 Oct 1880 in Godgestown, Kildare, Ireland and died after 1940 in Canada ??.

13. Mary Murphy, daughter of **John Murphy** and **Ellen Tobey,** was born in Aug 1844 in Ireland, died on 17 Apr 1916 in Mackinac County, Michigan at age 71, and was buried in Fenlons Cemetery.

> Research Notes: Michigan Deaths and Burials, 1800-1995
> Name:Mary Fenlon Gender:FemaleDeath Date:17 Apr 1916
> Death Place:Clark Twp., Mackinac, Michigan Age:72 Birth Date:1844 Birthplace: Ireland
> Occupation:Housewife Race:White Marital Status:Married Father's Name:John Murphy Mother's Name: Ellen Tobey

Mary married **Edward Fenlon** in 1855 in County Carlow, Ireland.

14. John C. Hintz, son of **Claus Nicolaus Hintz** and **Anna Margretha Everitt,** was born on 28 Jun 1822 in Mecklenburg, Germany, died on 25 May 1898 in Gros Cap, Mackinac County, Michigan at age 75, and was buried in Gros Cap Cemetery.

> Research Notes: Gros Cap Records: It is stated that at the time of the Civil War John Hintz had over $2,000 in gold in his home. He made arrangements for substitute soldiers during the war.

John married **Emilie W. Kroplien** in 1850 in Mecklenburg, Germany.

Children from this marriage were:

    i.   **Andrew F. Hintz** was born on 1 Aug 1852 in Mecklenburg, Germany, died in Apr 1865 in Mackinac County, Michigan at age 12, and was buried in Gros Cap Cemetery.

    ii.   **William Hintz** was born about 1855 in Moran, Mackinac County, Michigan and died on 8 Mar 1883 in Milwaukee, Wisconsin about age 28.

    iii.   **Bertha Hintz** was born on 26 Oct 1857 in Mackinac County, Michigan, died on 25 Oct 1887 in Mackinac County, Michigan at age 29, and was buried in Gros Cap Cemetery.

    iv.   **Emma Hintz** was born on 20 Jun 1860 in St Ignace, MacKinac County, Michigan and died on 30 Sep 1931 in St. Ignace, Mackinac County, Michigan at age 71.

    v.   **Henry H. Hintz** was born on 31 Jul 1863 in Mackinac County, Michigan, died on 29 Jul 1890 in Detroit, Wayne County, Michigan at age 26, and was buried in Gros Cap Cemetery.

    vi.   **Mary Hintz** was born on 31 Jul 1863 in Mackinac County, Michigan, died on 1 Mar 1938 in Detroit, Wayne County, Michigan at age 74, and was buried in Pine Hill Cemetery.

    vii.   **Carl F. Hintz** was born on 27 May 1865 in Mackinac County, Michigan, died on 4 May 1872 in Mackinac County, Michigan at age 6, and was buried in Gros Cap Cemetery.

7   viii.   **Emily Hintz**

15. Emilie W. Kroplien, daughter of **Carl Daniel Friedrich Kröplin** and **Caroline Marie Sophie,** was born on 12 Mar 1828 in Mecklenburg, Germany, died on 12 Oct 1901 in Mackinac County, Michigan at age 73, and was buried in Gros Cap Cemetery.

Emilie married **John C. Hintz** in 1850 in Mecklenburg, Germany.

Fifth Generation (2nd Great-Grandparents)

16. Archibald Blackburn McGrew, son of **James Blackburn Baird McGrew** and **Elizabeth McFerran,** was born on 26 Dec 1799 in Sewickley, Westmoreland County, Pennsylvania and died on 11 Jan 1843 in Sewickley, Westmoreland County, Pennsylvania at age 43.

Archibald married **Susannah Gilbert** on 26 Dec 1822 in Sewickley, Westmoreland County, Pennsylvania.

Children from this marriage were:

	i.	**Philena Wakefield McGrew** was born on 14 Oct 1823 in Westmoreland County, Pennsylvania and died on 15 Dec 1889 in Wesley Township, Washington, Ohio at age 66.
	ii.	**Abner Gilbert McGrew** was born on 27 Feb 1826 in Westmoreland County, Pennsylvania and died in Aug 1890 at age 64.
	iii.	**Elizabeth McGrew** was born on 11 Nov 1827 in Westmoreland County, Pennsylvania and died on 24 Jun 1900 in West Newton, Westmoreland, Pennsylvania at age 72.
	iv.	**Margaret Ann McGrew** was born on 19 Oct 1829 in Sewickley, Westmoreland, Pennsylvania and died on 10 Apr 1902 at age 72.
	v.	**Mary Jane McGrew** was born on 29 Jan 1832 in Sewickley, Westmoreland, Pennsylvania and died on 16 Sep 1908 in What Cheer, Keokuk, Iowa at age 76.
8	vi.	**Benjamin Gilbert McGrew**
	vii.	**Deborah McGrew** was born on 2 Jan 1836 in Westmoreland County, Pennsylvania and died in Jan 1902 in City, Guernsey, Ohio at age 66.
	viii.	**Isabella McGrew** was born on 29 Mar 1837 in Westmoreland County, Pennsylvania.
	ix.	**Rebecca McGrew** was born on 28 Aug 1838 in Westmoreland County, Pennsylvania and died on 7 Feb 1925 in West Newton, Westmoreland, Pennsylvania at age 86.
	x.	**Phebe Catherine McGrew** was born on 7 Jul 1840 in Westmoreland County, Pennsylvania and died on 31 Mar 1932 in Washington County, Ohio at age 91.
	xi.	**James McGrew** was born on 1 Mar 1842 in Westmoreland County, Pennsylvania and died on 31 Dec 1842 in Westmoreland County, Pennsylvania.

17. Susannah Gilbert, daughter of **Abner Gilbert** and **Ann Cooper,** was born on 12 Mar 1804 in Sewickley, Westmoreland County, Pennsylvania and died on 14 Sep 1873 in Allegheny County, Pennsylvania at age 69.

Susannah married **Archibald Blackburn McGrew** on 26 Dec 1822 in Sewickley, Westmoreland County, Pennsylvania.

18. John Arnold Howell, son of **William Howell** and **Rebecka,** was born on 31 Jan 1811 in Pennsylvania, died on 28 Aug 1869 in North Huntingdon Township, Westmoreland County, Pennsylvania at age 58, and was buried in Long Run Presbyterian Cemetery.

John married **Sarah Sowash**.

Children from this marriage were:

	i.	**Maria Howell** was born in 1836 in Allegheny County, Pennsylvania.
	ii.	**David Howell** was born in 1837 in Allegheny County, Pennsylvania.
9	iii.	**Katherine Sowash "Kate" Howell**
	iv.	**Anna Eliza Howell** was born in 1843 in Allegheny County, Pennsylvania.

19. Sarah Sowash, daughter of **John Sowash** and **Catherine Thomas,** was born on 7 Apr 1808 in Allegheny County, Pennsylvania, died on 21 Jul 1878 in North Huntingdon Township, Westmoreland County, Pennsylvania at age 70, and was buried in Long Run Presbyterian Cemetery.

Research Notes: Sarah married first Jacob Poist, by which she might have had one child before his death. Then she married John Howell.

Sarah married **John Arnold Howell**.

20. Abraham Leasure, son of **Daniel Leasure** and **Elizabeth Reynolds,** was born on 19 Jun 1786 in Greensburg, Westmoreland County, Pennsylvania, died on 29 Apr 1839 in Hempfield Township, Westmoreland County, Pennsylvania at age 52, and was buried in Sewickley Union Cemetery Association.

Abraham married **Barbara Anna Lobingier**.

The child from this marriage was:

10	i.	**Rev. Loren Bigelow Leasure**

21. Barbara Anna Lobingier, daughter of **Christopher Lobingier Jr.** and **Elizabeth Mueller,** was born on 22 Feb 1786 in Laurelville, Westmoreland County, Pennsylvania, died on 6 Apr 1863 in Hempfield Township, Westmoreland County, Pennsylvania at age 77, and was buried in Sewickley Union Cemetery Association.

Barbara married **Abraham Leasure**.

22. John Tintsman, son of **John Tintsman/Dinstman** and **Frances Stauffer,** was born on 1 Jul 1812 in Westmoreland County, Pennsylvania, died on 29 Mar 1866 in Westmoreland County, Pennsylvania at age 53, and was buried in Mount Pleasant, Westmoreland County, Pennsylvania.

John married **Anna Stauffer Overholt**.

The child from this marriage was:

11	i.	**Anna Overholt Tintsman**

23. Anna Stauffer Overholt, daughter of **Abraham Overholt** and **Maria Stauffer,** was born on 4 Jul 1812 in Westoverton, Pennsylvania and died on 29 Mar 1866 in Fayette City, Fayette County, Pennsylvania at age 53.

Anna married **John Tintsman**.

24. John Fenlon was born in 1801, died in 1866 in County Carlow, Ireland at age 65, and was buried in St. Mary's Church of Ireland Church Cemetery unmarked.

Research Notes: John Fenlon
Ireland Civil Registration Indexes, 1845-1958

Name:
John Fenlon,Event Type: Death, Event Date:1866 Event Place:Carlow, Ireland
Registration Quarter and Year:1866 Registration District: Carlow Age:65
Birth Year (Estimated):   1801
Volume Number:3

John Fenlon
Ireland, Petty Sessions Court Registers, 1828-1912

Name:John Fenlon
Event Type:Court
Event Date 29 Oct 1860
Event Place:Carlow, Ireland
County: Carlow
Role of Individual:Witness
Court: Bagenalstown

John married **Ellen Scott**.

Children from this marriage were:

	i.	**James Fenlon** was born in County Carlow, Ireland.
12	ii.	**Edward Fenlon**
	iii.	**Elizabeth Fenlon** was born about 1827 in County Carlow, Ireland.

25. Ellen Scott was born in 1801, died in Apr 1881 in County Carlow, Ireland at age 80, and was buried in St. Mary's Church of Ireland Church Cemetery unmarked.

Research Notes: Ireland Civil Registration Indexes, 1845-1958

Ellen married **John Fenlon**.

26. John Murphy was born in 1791 in Ireland and died in 1871 in County Carlow, Ireland at age 80.

Research Notes: Ireland Civil Registration Indexes, 1845-1958
Name: John Murphy Event Type: Death Event Date: 1871 Event Place: Carlow, Ireland
Registration Quarter and Year:1871 Registration District:Carlow
Age:80 Birth Year (Estimated):1791
Volume Number:3

John married **Ellen Tobey**.

The child from this marriage was:

13	i.	**Mary Murphy**

27. Ellen Tobey was born in 1829 in Ireland and died in Jan-Mar 1900 in County Carlow, Ireland at age 71.

Research Notes: Ireland Civil Registration Indexes, 1845-1958
Name: Ellen Murphy Event Type Death Event Date: Jan - Mar 1900
Event Place: Carlow, Ireland Registration Quarter and Year: Jan - Mar 1900
Registration District:Carlow Age:70 Birth Year (Estimated):1829 Volume Number
3

Ellen married **John Murphy**.

28. Claus Nicolaus Hintz, son of **Johann Hintz** and **Alheit Mullern,** was born on 26 Dec 1788 in Lamstedt, Hannover, Prussia, Germany, was christened on 26 Dec 1788 in Lamstedt Kr Neuhaus, Hannover, Preußen, Germany, and died on 21 Apr 1871 in Sankt Wendel, Rhein, Preußen, Germany at age 82.

Research Notes: Birth and DSeath from Deutschland, Rheinland, Bistum Trier, katholische Kirchenbücher, 1704-1957

Claus married **Anna Margretha Everitt.**

The child from this marriage was:

    14   i.   **John C. Hintz**

29. Anna Margretha Everitt, daughter of **Johann Hermann Everitt** and **Anna Margretha Everts,** was born on 19 Apr 1789 in EVANGELISCH, STAPELAGE, LIPPE, GERMANY and died on 27 Aug 1866 in Rhein, Preußen, Germany at age 77.

Research Notes: Birth and DSeath from Deutschland, Rheinland, Bistum Trier, katholische Kirchenbücher, 1704-1957

Anna married **Claus Nicolaus Hintz.**

30. Carl Daniel Friedrich Kröplin.

Carl married **Caroline Marie Sophie.**

The child from this marriage was:

    15   i.   **Emilie W. Kroplien**

31. Caroline Marie Sophie.

Caroline married **Carl Daniel Friedrich Kröplin.**

Sixth Generation (3rd Great-Grandparents)

32. James Blackburn Baird McGrew, son of **James McGrew** and **Mary Dicks,** was born on 25 Aug 1751 in Petersburg, York County, Pennsylvania, died on 11 Jun 1818 in Sewickley, Westmoreland County, Pennsylvania at age 66, and was buried in Friends Burial Ground.

James married **Elizabeth McFerran** on 1 Jan 1774 in Virginia.

Children from this marriage were:

    i.   **James Blackburn McGrew** was born on 21 Mar 1781 in Adams County, Pennsylvania, died on 4 Oct 1836 in West Newton, Westmoreland, Pennsylvania at age 55, and was buried in Friends Burial Ground.

    ii.   **Deborah McGrew** was born on 6 Sep 1783 in Adams County, Pennsylvania, died on 16 Aug 1855 in Fayette City, Fayette County, Pennsylvania at age 71, and was buried in Friends Burial Ground.

    iii.   **Simon Blackburn McGrew** was born on 14 Feb 1788 in York County, Pennsylvania, died on 9 Oct 1854 in Westmoreland County, Pennsylvania at age 66, and was buried in Friends Burial Ground.

    iv.   **Thomas Blackburn McGrew** was born on 11 Mar 1792 in York County, Pennsylvania, died on 10 Mar 1857 in Hamilton County, Ohio at age 64, and was buried in Wesleyan Cemetery.

    v.   **Dr. John Blackburn McGrew** was born on 7 May 1795 in Westmoreland County, Pennsylvania, died in 1865 in Harrison County, Ohio at age 70, and was buried in Longview Cemetery.

    16   vi.   **Archibald Blackburn McGrew**

33. Elizabeth McFerran, daughter of **John McFerran** and **Martha Sterling,** was born on 1 Nov 1755 in York County, Pennsylvania and died on 10 Feb 1823 in Sewickley, Westmoreland County, Pennsylvania at age 67.

Elizabeth married **James Blackburn Baird McGrew** on 1 Jan 1774 in Virginia.

34. Abner Gilbert, son of **Benjamin Gilbert** and **Elizabeth Peart,** was born on 2 Mar 1765 in Philadelphia County, Pennsylvania and died on 31 May 1831 in Providence, at age 66.

Abner married **Ann Cooper** on 18 Jan 1799 in Westmoreland County, Pennsylvania.

The child from this marriage was:

17   i.   **Susannah Gilbert**

35. Ann Cooper was born on 7 Jul 1768 in Sadsbury, Lancaster County, Pennsylvania and died on 13 Nov 1845 in Sewickley, Westmoreland County, Pennsylvania at age 77.

Ann married **Abner Gilbert** on 18 Jan 1799 in Westmoreland County, Pennsylvania.

36. William Howell, son of **John Howell** and **Jenetta Catherine Morgan,** was born in 1756 in Llandeilo, Carmarthenshire, Wales and died on 11 Feb 1827 in North Huntingdon Township, Westmoreland County, Pennsylvania at age 71.

William married **Rebecka**.

Children from this marriage were:

     i.   **Aaron Howell** was born in 1809 in New Jersey and died on 27 Aug 1881 in North Huntingdon, Westmoreland, Pennsylvania at age 72.

18   ii.   **John Arnold Howell**

37. Rebecka was born about 1771.

Rebecka married **William Howell**.

38. John Sowash, son of **Henry Sowash** and **Maria Anna Esther Schneider,** was born in 1762 in Berks County, Pennsylvania, died on 3 Dec 1827 in Irwin, Westmoreland County, Pennsylvania at age 65, and was buried in Berks County, Pennsylvania.

Research Notes: John Sowash, Sr., son of Henry and Anna Esther (Schneider) Sowash

John Sowash, Sr. was born in Rockland Township, Berks County, Pennsylvania, about 1765. According to History of Westmoreland County he was born in Maryland.

He married Catherine Thomas in Westmoreland County, Pennsylvania. the daughter of Garret/Gearhardt and Mary Magdalene Thomas'

He was a soldier in the Revolutionary war, a lieutenant in the militia. In church connections, he was a Methodist.

He and Catherine Sowash were the parents of 15 children, of whom three died young. Those attaining maturity were: Garrett, John, Joseph, David, Jacob, George, Elizabeth, Catherine, Sarah, Ann, Hannah, and Rachel."

John married **Catherine Thomas**.

The child from this marriage was:

19   i.   **Sarah Sowash**

39. Catherine Thomas, daughter of **Heinrich Gerhard (Garrett) Thomas** and **Magdalena,** was born on 2 Aug 1770 in Elizabeth Township, Lancaster County, Pennsylvania, died on 4 Aug 1851 in Irwin, Westmoreland County, Pennsylvania at age 81, and was buried in Brush Creek Cemetery.

Research Notes: She was the daughter of Heinrich Gerhard (Garrett) Thomas and Magdalena (________)Thomas. Catherine's sister Eve (Thomas) Weber was the mother of Maria M. Weber who married John Sowash, Sr.'s nephew Isaac Sowash.

Catherine married **John Sowash**.

40. Daniel Leasure, son of **Abraham Leasure** and **Margaret Marshall,** was born in 1758 in York County, Pennsylvania, died on 9 Dec 1830 in Mount Pleasant, Westmoreland County, Pennsylvania at age 72, and was buried in Middle Presbyterian Cemetery.

Research Notes: Died-On the 8th inst, at his residence in Mount Pleasant township, Mr. DANIEL LEASURE, at an advanced age.

From: The Greensburg Gazette, Greensburg, Pennsylvania, on Friday December 17, 1830, Page 3

Note: Paper says he died the 8th and the headstone says the 9th.

Married: Elizabeth Ryan, about 1783

Daniel married **Elizabeth Reynolds** in 1783.

The child from this marriage was:

    20   i.   **Abraham Leasure**

41. Elizabeth Reynolds, daughter of **Joshua Reynolds** and **Rachel Kilgore,** was born in 1768, died on 5 Sep 1840 in Mount Pleasant, Westmoreland County, Pennsylvania at age 72, and was buried in Middle Presbyterian Cemetery.

Elizabeth married **Daniel Leasure** in 1783.

42. Christopher Lobingier Jr., son of **Christopher Lobingier** and **Anna Catherine Hubele,** was born on 4 Oct 1741 in Lancaster County, Pennsylvania, died on 4 Jul 1798 in Mount Pleasant, Westmoreland County, Pennsylvania at age 56, and was buried in Ridge Churches Union Cemetery.

Christopher married **Elizabeth Mueller**.

The child from this marriage was:

    21   i.   **Barbara Anna Lobingier**

43. Elizabeth Mueller, daughter of **Captain John George Mueller** and **Barbara Gloninger,** was born on 13 Jun 1744, died on 6 Sep 1815 in Stoystown, Somerset County, Pennsylvania at age 71, and was buried in IOOF Cemetery.

Elizabeth married **Christopher Lobingier Jr.**

44. John Tintsman/Dinstman, son of **Adam Tintsman/Dinstman** and **Elizabeth Anna Wismer,** was born on 21 Aug 1778 in Bucks County, Pennsylvania and died on 8 May 1849 in Harmony, Susquehanna, Pennsylvania at age 70.

John married **Frances Stauffer**.

Children from this marriage were:

        i.   **Anna F. Tintsman** was born in 1806 in Westmoreland County, Pennsylvania and died in 1881 in Adams County, Illinois at age 75.
    22   ii.   **John Tintsman**

45. Frances Stauffer, daughter of **Abraham Stauffer** and **Anna Nissley,** was born on 6 Apr 1783 in Bucks County, Pennsylvania and died on 27 May 1869 in Beaver, Mahoning, Ohio at age 86.

Frances married **John Tintsman/Dinstman**.

46. Abraham Overholt, son of **Heinrich Oberholtzer** and **Anna Beitler,** was born on 19 Apr 1784 in Bucks County, Pennsylvania and died on 15 Jan 1870 in East Huntingdon twp, Westmoreland County, Pennsylvania at age 85.

Abraham married **Maria Stauffer**.

Children from this marriage were:

    23   i.   **Anna Stauffer Overholt**
        ii.   **Aaron Overholt**
        iii.   **Elizabeth Stauffer Overholt** was born on 2 Jun 1819 in Westmoreland County, Pennsylvania and died on 1 Oct 1905 in Wooster, Wayne, Ohio at age 86.

47. Maria Stauffer was born on 13 Jul 1791 in Fayette City, Fayette, Pennsylvania and died on 1 Nov 1874 in East Huntingdon, Westmoreland County, Pennsylvania at age 83.

Maria married **Abraham Overholt**.

56. Johann Hintz.

Johann married **Alheit Mullern**.

The child from this marriage was:

    28   i.   **Claus Nicolaus Hintz**

57. Alheit Mullern.

Alheit married **Johann Hintz**.

58. Johann Hermann Everitt.

Johann married **Anna Margretha Everts**.

The child from this marriage was:

    29   i.   **Anna Margretha Everitt**

59. Anna Margretha Everts.

Anna married **Johann Hermann Everitt**.

Seventh Generation (4th Great-Grandparents)

64. James McGrew was born on 8 Oct 1707 in Omagh, County Tyrone, Ireland and died after 1792 in York County, Pennsylvania.

Research Notes: James McGrew was born about 1707 to Robert McGrew and his wife, Isabella.

He married Mary Dicks on Mar. 25, 1735 at Holy Trinity (Old Swedes) Church in Wilmington, Delaware.[1]

James was assessed in London Grove, Chester County, Pennsylvania in 1729 and 1734.

James and his wife brought a certificate from Hopewell, Virginia to Warrington Monthly Meeting in 1750.[2]

The births of their children were recorded at the Menallen Monthly Meeting.[3]

Children

Holy Trinity (Old Swedes) Church in Wilmington, Delaware

Finley b. 1st mo. [Mar] 13, 1735, m. Dinah Cox; and removed about 1787 to the Redstone region of Pennsylvania
Deborah b. 7th mo. [Sep] 14, 1739 m. Joseph Blackburn in 1758
Ann b. 4th mo. [Jun] 29, 1741, m. Elijah Newlin
Nathan, b. 3rd mo. [May] 10 1743, d. 1769 m. Rachel Blackburn in 1767
Simeon b. 11th mo. [Jan] 5, 1745/6, m. Martha McKnight
Mary b. 11th mo. [Jan] 5 1748/9, m. Moses Blackburn in 1767
James b. 6th mo. [Aug] 25 1751 m. Elizabeth McFerran about 1774 and removed to the Redstone region about 1794

The Will of James McGrew filed in York County, Pennsylvania

In the name of God Amen I James McGrew of Menallin Township in the County of York and State of Pennsylvania, being weak in Body but of Perfect mind and Memory, blessed be Almighty God for the same calling to mind the mortality of Body and that it is appointed for all men once to die, do make and Publish this my last will and Testament in the manner and form following that is to say principally and first of all give and Recommend my soul to Almighty God who gave it, and my body to the earth to be buried in a decent and Christian manner at discretion of my Executors as will be hereafter named and as touching such worldly Estate wherewith it pleased God to bless me with in this life I give and dispose of the same in the following manner viz first,

I order that all my just debts and funeral expenses be discharged and paid. Then I give and bequeath unto my youngest son James McGrew all my real estate in Lands lying and being in Menallen Township, York County and State aforesaid on which I am now living to him his heirs, Executors, Administrators and Assigns forever.

Also I give and bequeath to my said son James two chairs and one table, and griddle and pair of Stilyards and a frying pan also all the farming utensils that belongs to the said farm.

I also allow my son James McGrew to pay the sum of Forty Pounds to my son Simeon McGrew to be paid out of my real estate to be paid in Gold or Silver to be paid in Eighteen months after my decease.

Also I give and bequeath to my well beloved son Simeon McGrew the sum of Forty Pounds in Gold or Silver also my fine hat and Saddle which is to be paid out of my Personal Estate and to be paid Eighteen months after my Decease, this shall be his full share and no more being in part already advanced.

Also I give and bequeath to my beloved son Finley McGrew the sum of three Pounds in Gold or Silver (I also allow my son Finley my Riding rein and greatcoat and strait bodied coat) to be paid out of the Personal Estate to be paid in Eighteen months after my Decease. This shall be his full share and no more being in part already advanced.

Also I give and bequeath to my well beloved Daughter Deborah Blackburn, wife of Joseph Blackburn, deceased, the Sum of Twenty Pounds in Gold or Silver to be paid Eighteen months after my Decease, exclusive of what she has already received.

Also I give and bequeath to my Granddaughter Mary Brandon, the sum of three Pounds in Gold or Silver to be paid out of my

Personal Estate Eighteen months after my Decease.

Also I give and bequeath to my three daughters, viz, Deborah, Ann and Mary all the remainder of my personal estate after the legacies already mentioned to be divided equally between the three.

Also I give and bequeath to Sarah Kelsey wife of Joseph Kelsey my bed and bedding.

Also I give and bequeath to my Grand Daughter Jean McGrew, daughter of James McGrew one case of Drawers.

And lastly I do constitute and appoint my aforesaid son James McGrew and my nephew Alexander McGrew my whole and Sole Executors to see the orderly accomplishments of this my last will and Testament according to the true intent and meaning thereof also to pay and settle all said Legacies in Eighteen months after my decease. In confirmation whereof I have hereunto set my Hand and Seal this Nineteenth Day of December in the year of our Lord one thousand seven hundred and ninety two, 1792.

James McGrew (X His Mark)

Signed, Sealed and Pronounced and Declared as my Last will and testament in presence of Archibald McGrew, Wm. McGrew

Sources Records of Holy Trinity (Old Swedes) Church, Wilmington, Del., from 1697 to 1773; pg. 359.
? Immigration of the Irish Quakers into Pennsylvania in York County, Established in 1747 from Sadsbury. "James McGrew, kinsman doubtless of Finley McGrew, brought a certificate for himself and wife from Hopewell, Va to Warrington Monthly Meeting in 1750. A James Magrew probably the same, was assessed in London Grove, Chester County in 1729 and 1734. Children of James and Mary McGrew; Finley b. Jan 13, 1736, m. Dinah Cox; and removed about 1787 to the Redstone region of Pennsylvania; Deborah b. Jul 14, 1739 m. Joseph Blackburn in 1758; Ann b. Apr 29, 1741, m. ? Newlin; Nathan, B. Mar 10 1743, d. 1769 m. Rachel Blackburn in 1767; Simon b. Nov 5, 1745, Mary b. Nov 5 1748, m. Moses Blackburn in 1767, James b. Jun 25 1751 m. Elizabeth McFerran, (p381) about 1774 and removed to the Redstone region about 1794. Children of James and Elizabeth McFerran McGrew; Mary b. May 10 1774, m. Joel Hutton; Nathan m. Elizabeth Winder; Jane; James B. Deborah m. Samuel McGrew; Joseph; Simon; Finley; Thomas; John B; Jacob; Archibald m. Susanna Gilbert.
? Swarthmore College; Swarthmore, Pennsylvania; Minutes and Deaths 1785-1884; Collection: Baltimore Yearly Meeting Minutes; Call Number: RG2/B/M461 3.1; Menallen Monthly Meeting; Minutes and Deaths 1785-1884; pg. 35.

James married **Mary Dicks** on 25 Mar 1735 in Willmington, Newcastle County Delaware.

The child from this marriage was:

    32   i.   **James Blackburn Baird McGrew**

65. Mary Dicks was born about 1715.

Research Notes: Mary (Dicks) McGrew is believed to be the daughter of Nathan and Deborah (Clark) Dicks. She married James McGrew at Old Swedes Church. Mary and James are buried in Friends Grove Burial Ground, Butler Township, Adams, PA.

Mary married **James McGrew** on 25 Mar 1735 in Willmington, Newcastle County Delaware.

66. John McFerran was born in 1698 in Ballymaconnell, County Down, Ireland and died 20 Nov 1778 to 1780 in Petersburg, Penn Township, Now Perry, Pennsylvania at age 80.

Research Notes: History of Whiteside County, Illinois by William W. Davis

John married **Martha Sterling** in 1735 in New Jersey.

The child from this marriage was:

    33   i.   **Elizabeth McFerran**

67. Martha Sterling was born in 1707 in Ireland and died in 1780 in Petersburg, Penn Township, Now Perry, Pennsylvania at age 73.

Martha married **John McFerran** in 1735 in New Jersey.

68. Benjamin Gilbert, son of **Joseph John Gilbert** and **Sarah James,** was born circa 1711 in Philadelphia County, Pennsylvania and died on 8 Jun 1780 in St. Lawrence River, Ontario, Canada about age 69.

Research Notes: On the 25th of April, 1780, eleven Indians entered his house, tied up him and his family, and robbed his house.

The plunder was put on two of his horses. The buildings were set afire and the hostages marched through the wilderness until they reached Niagara one month later. Benjamin, his wife and son Jesse were surrendered to Colonel Johnson but the others were retained. While being returned via open boats on the St. Lawrence River, Benjamin died in a heavy rain on the eighth of June, 1780 of an illness he acquired before their departure. He was buried under an oak tree along the river. His wife and son returned home and the rest of the captives were finally released and returned to Byberry on the 29th of September, 1782.

Benjamin married **Elizabeth Peart** in 1760 in Philadelphia County, Pennsylvania.

The child from this marriage was:

    34   i.   **Abner Gilbert**

69. Elizabeth Peart was born on 27 Mar 1725 in Philadelphia County, Pennsylvania and died on 5 Aug 1810 in Fallowfield Township, Washington County, Pennsylvania at age 85.

Elizabeth married **Benjamin Gilbert** in 1760 in Philadelphia County, Pennsylvania.

72. John Howell, son of **Thomas Howell** and **Martha Williams,** was born on 3 Aug 1726 in Llangyniew, Powys, Wales and died on 17 Oct 1801 in Shirley, Huntingdon, Pennsylvania at age 75.

John married **Jenetta Catherine Morgan**.

The child from this marriage was:

    36   i.   **William Howell**

73. Jenetta Catherine Morgan, daughter of **John Bevan Morgan** and **Catherine David,** was born about 1725 in Ystradgynlais, Powys, Wales and died in Jun 1817 in Thornbury, Gloucestershire, England about age 92.

Jenetta married **John Howell**.

76. Henry Sowash, son of **Johannes H. Sauvage** and **Susanna,** was born in 1731 in Alsace, died in 1799 in Westmoreland County, Pennsylvania at age 68, and was buried in Brush Creek Cemetery.

    Research Notes: His will was proven on June 10, 1799 so his Date of Death was prior to that.

    There is no record of his actual burial in Brush Creek Cemetery, but it is probable since other family members were buried there. The Revolutionary War marker was placed beside the site of John Sowash's burial. -information provided by Richard Soash #47678170

    Since Henry was not naturalized when he arrived with his father, he was under the age of 16 in 1738. He was probably born in Alsace, then a part of Germany. This area between France and Germany has gone back and forth between the two countries for centuries as a result of war. Many French fled Catholic France for Protestant Germany after the Edict of Nantes was revoked in 1685, revoking the rights of religious freedom to the Huguenots in France.

    Henry married Maria Anna Esther Schneider on 27 Nov 1749 at Mertz Church in Berks County, PA.

    Henry Showash was listed in the Rockland Township, Berks County tax list in 1757 (History of the County of Berks and Lebanon, Rupps, 1844, p.243).

    Henry was listed in the 1767 Berks Co., PA. tax list in Rockland Township, owning 150 acres, two horses, two cattle, and four sheep (PA. Archives, Third Series, Vol. XVIII, p. 10).
    In 1768 Henry paid taxes on the same property, except he no longer had the cattle and only claimed 100 acres of land (PA. Archives, Third Series, Vol. XVII, p. 10).

    Henrich and Esther Sowasche served as sponsors for Anna Elisabetha Falck, born 28 Apr, baptized 10 May 1772 at Christ (or Mertz) Church on Bieber Creek in Rockland Twp., Berks Co., PA. Anna's parents were listed as Christoph and Maria Elisabetha Falck. Maria was their daughter who married Chrisopher Faulk.

    Henry and his son Daniel Sowasch enlisted in Captain Daniel Eyester's [Heister ?] Company in September 1776 until January 1777 in the Jerseys to fight in the Revolutionary War (PA. Archives, Sixth Series, Vol. II, p. 601).

In the 1779 Berks County tax list, Henry had 150 acres, two horses and three cattle. His son Daniel was also listed in this tax list with no property.

Henry does not appear in 1780 tax list though he still owned land.
Sometime between 1779 and 1783, Henry's wife Maria Anna Esther died as Henry was listed as a widower in a 1783 deed record (p.471) At this time he sold his land in Berks County as he is listed as "Henry Sowass of the State of Virginia, Widower." Jacob Gaumer, son-in-law of Henry, and Henry were both listed in the 1782 tax list of Berkeley County, Virginia (now West Virginia). Two of his other daughters Johanna Elizabeth (Sowash) Faulk and Susanna (Sowash) DeLong also seem to have moved to Berkelely County.

Henry appeared in the Derry Township, Westmoreland County, Pennsylvania, tax list of 1786. Henry seems to be with his son Daniel in Rostraver Township, Westmoreland County in the first U.S. Census of 1790.

Henry made his will on 07 May 1795 which was probated in Westmoreland County on 10 Jun 1799 (Bk 1, p. 151). No record of burial has been located. It seems highly probable that he was buried in Brush Creek Cemetery in Westmoreland County, PA. A gravestone was erected by the Sauvage/Sowash/Soash Family Association in Brush Creek Cemetery.

Bio by: Richard Soash

Henry married **Maria Anna Esther Schneider**.

The child from this marriage was:

    38   i.   **John Sowash**

77. Maria Anna Esther Schneider died in Berks County, Pennsylvania and was buried in Sauvage Family Graveyard.

Research Notes: Maria died between 1782 and 1783. Although not proven, she was probably buried in this vacated graveyard before her husband Henry Sowash moved to Berkley County, Virginia (now West Virginia).

Maria married **Henry Sowash**.

78. Heinrich Gerhard (Garrett) Thomas.

Heinrich married **Magdalena**.

The child from this marriage was:

    39   i.   **Catherine Thomas**

79. Magdalena.

Magdalena married **Heinrich Gerhard (Garrett) Thomas**.

80. Abraham Leasure, son of **Abraham Leasure** and **Margarette Poinsett,** was born in Feb 1713 in Basel, Basel-Stadt, Basel-Stadt, Switzerland, died on 15 Mar 1803 in Leasureville, Butler County, Pennsylvania at age 90, and was buried in Unity Cemetery.

Research Notes: easure, — The Leasure family is both ancient and honorable, and was originally seated in the province of Navarre. At the Revocation a branch of this family was compelled to flee to Switzerland for safety, and from whence came Abraham Leasure, who arrived in 1754, and located in upper Dauphin county, where the family name is still extant. A son of the immigrant located in Westmoreland county where his descendants became prominent, notably General Daniel Leasure, a distinguished officer of the Civil war.

Abraham married **Margaret Marshall**.

The child from this marriage was:

    40   i.   **Daniel Leasure**

81. Margaret Marshall was born in 1715 in France, died on 15 Mar 1818 in Westmoreland County, Pennsylvania at age 103, and was buried in Unity Cemetery.

Margaret married **Abraham Leasure**.

82. Joshua Reynolds was born circa 1730, died on 6 Oct 1805 in Mount Pleasant, Westmoreland County, Pennsylvania about age 75, and was buried in Middle Presbyterian Cemetery.

Joshua married **Rachel Kilgore**.

The child from this marriage was:

    41   i.   **Elizabeth Reynolds**

83. Rachel Kilgore died on 20 Dec 1848 in Mount Pleasant, Westmoreland County, Pennsylvania and was buried in Middle Presbyterian Cemetery.

Rachel married **Joshua Reynolds**.

84. Christopher Lobingier was born circa 1700 in Wittenberg, Germany and died circa 1772 in Hummelstown, Dauphin County, Pennsylvania about age 72.

    Research Notes: Source: Vince Gerheim . According to this source, Christopher LOBINGER immigrated to Philadelphia on September 18, 1727 on the ship William and Sara[h]. If this source is correct, then Christopher's surname, as reported on the ship's passenger list, was either LABENGYGER or LAMBENGYGER. See the ship's passenger lists cited below.

    (2) Immigrants in Pennsylvania from 1727 to 1776 [database online], Provo, UT: Ancestry.com, 2001:

    At a meeting of the Board of the Provincial Council, held at the Court House in Philadelphia, Sept. 21, 1727, one hundred and nine Palatines appeared, who, with their families, numbered about four hundred persons. These were imported into the Province in the ship William and Sarah, William Hill, Master, from Rotterdam, last from Dover, England, as by clearance from the officers of His Majesty's customs there. The said Master being asked if he had any license from the Court of Great Britain for transporting those people, and what their intentions were in coming hither, said that he had no license or allowance for their transportation other than the above clearance, and that he believed they designed to settle in this Province.--Col. Rec. III. 283.

    ID Number: MH:N750

    MH:I2875

    N726All male persons above the age of sixteen did repeat and subscribe their names, or made their mark, to the following Declaration: "We subscribers, natives and late inhabitants of the Palatinate upon the Rhine and places adjacent, having transported ourselves and families into this Province of Pennsylvania, a colony subject to the crown of Great Britain, in hopes and expectation of finding a retreat and peaceable settlement therein, Do solemnly promise and engage, that we will be faithful and bear true allegiance to His present Majesty, King George THE SECOND, and His successors, kings of GreatBritain, and will be faithful to the proprietor of this Province; and that we will demean ourselves peaceably to all His said Majesty 's subjects, and strictly observe and conform to the Laws of England and of this Province, to the utmost of our power and the best of our understanding." . . .

    In vol. iii. 284. Colonial Records, it is stated, "sundry of these foreigners lying sick on board, never came to be qualified." I have compared Lists A, B and C and find in List A, besides those givenabove, the following names: . . .

    Christopher Labengyger, name written by clerk

    ID Number: MH:N751

    MH:I2875

    N727(3) The Olive Tree Genealogy :

    Palatine Ship WILLIAM AND SARAH 1727

    William Hill, Master from Rotterdam, to Philadelphia 18th Sept. 1727

    Name: Christopher Lambengyger

    # persons in party: 2

    ID Number: MH:N752

    MH:I2875

    N728(4) Boucher, John Newton, A Century and a Half of Pittsburg[h] and Her People, New York, NY: Lewis Publishing Company, 1908, vol. 3, p. 229:

    Christopher Lobingier, Sr. . . . was the founder of the family in this country. He with his brother Jacob emigrated from Wittenberg, Germany, prior to 1735, settling at Hummelstown, which was then in the territory embraced within Lancaster county, Pennsylvania, but which is now located in Dauphin county. The tradition in the family is that he was of French extraction, his forebears having been driven from France during the Huguenot persecution. They sought a refuge in Germany, and it was from that country that Christopher Lobingier and his brother started to found new homes in America. Soon after his arrival in this country Jacob disappeared while fighting the Indians and all trace of him was lost, the supposition being that he was killed by the savages. Christopher became an influential citizen and died where he located on his arrival in this country: He was buried in the old churchyard at Hummelstown, where his grave is still to be found, together with other members of his family.

    ID Number: MH:N753

MH:I2875

N729(4) Boucher, John N., History of Westmoreland County, Pennsylvania, New York, NY: Lewis Publishing Co., 1906: Vol. 2, p. 64: Christopher Lobingier . . . came from Mecklenberg, Germany, and settled in [Lancaster now] Dauphin county. He was married before leaving Germany. Little is known of him except that he was a farmer, and that both he and his wife died, and are buried in Dauphin county. They had one son, Christopher. . . .Vol. 2, p. 485: Christopher Lobingier . . . came from Mecklenburg, Germany, and settled in [Lancaster now] Dauphin county, Pennsylvania. Vol. 3, p. 298: Christopher Lobingier, Sr. . . . was the founder of this family in the United States. He was a native of Wittenberg, Germany, and emigrated with his brother Jacob from the Fatherland prior to 1735, settling in Harrisburg, Lancaster county, Pennsylvania.

[Note by compiler: This source is ambiguous as to the birthplace of Christopher LOBINGIER. In several places, this source states that Christopher "came from Mecklenburg;" this could mean that (1) Christopher was born there or (2) Christopher was there before he came to America. In another place, this source states that Christopher "was a native of Wittenberg." Mecklenburg is a populated place in Mecklenburg-Vorpommern, Germany; and Wittenberg is a populated place in Baden-Württemberg, Germany.]

Christopher married **Anna Catherine Hubele**.

The child from this marriage was:

    42   i.   **Christopher Lobingier Jr.**

85. Anna Catherine Hubele.

Anna married **Christopher Lobingier**.

86. Captain John George Mueller was born in 1715 in Sw Zurich, Switzerland and died in 1765 in Lebanon township, Pennsylvania at age 50.

Research Notes: Title: Commemorative biographical encyclopedia of Dauphin County, Pennsylvania: containing sketches of prominent and representative citizens, and many of the early Scotch-Irish and German settlers.
Authors: Anonymous
City of Publication: Chambersburg, Pa.
Publisher: J.M. Runk
Date: 1896
Page Count: 1223
Notes: "In the compilation of the biographies we were ably assisted by William H. Egle ... A.S. Dudley ... Harry I. Huber ... R.H. Schively."
Includes index.
ports. ;
Reel/Fiche Number: Genealogy & local history; LH 975
Subject Headings: Dauphin County (Pa.) -- Biography.
Pennsylvania -- Dauphin County

Biographical Encyclopedia of Dauphin County - found on page 171

Muller, John George, son of Rudolph Muller (more frequently writer Miller), was born September 21, 1715, in the Canton of Zurich, Switzerland; emigrated with his family to America in 1752, and settled in Lebanon township, Lancaster county, Province of Pennsylvania. He took the oath of allegiance October 23, 1752. He had been an officer in the Swiss service, and when the French and Indian war broke out he was commissioned a lieutenant in Col. James Burd's regiment of Provincial forces, May 8, 1760 (see Penn'a Arch. 2d ser., vol. ii, p605), promoted to a captaincy on the northern frontiers. October 12, 1764 (ib. p. 615). Captain Muller died April 19, 1765, in Lebanon township, leaving a wife Barbara Gloninger, who survived her husband several years, dying in 1783.

John married **Barbara Gloninger**.

The child from this marriage was:

    43   i.   **Elizabeth Mueller**

87. Barbara Gloninger.

Barbara married **Captain John George Mueller**.

88. Adam Tintsman/Dinstman, son of **Matthias Tintsman/Dinstman** and **Aylse,** was born in 1746 in Germany and died before 1813 in Westmoreland County, Pennsylvania.

Adam married **Elizabeth Anna Wismer**.

The child from this marriage was:

    44   i.   **John Tintsman/Dinstman**

89. Elizabeth Anna Wismer was born circa 1750 and died on 18 Oct 1824 in Westmoreland County, Pennsylvania about age 74.

Elizabeth married **Adam Tintsman/Dinstman**.

90. Abraham Stauffer was born in 1752 in Lancaster County, Pennsylvania and died on 3 Sep 1826 in Tyrone, Fayette County, Pennsylvania at age 74.

Abraham married **Anna Nissley**.

The child from this marriage was:

    45   i.   **Frances Stauffer**

91. Anna Nissley was born on 20 Sep 1752 in Lancaster County, Pennsylvania and died in 1817 in Tyrone, Fayette County, Pennsylvania at age 65.

Anna married **Abraham Stauffer**.

92. Heinrich Oberholtzer, son of **Martin Oberholtzer** and **Agnes Fretz,** was born on 5 Feb 1739 in Bucks County, Pennsylvania and died on 5 Mar 1813 in Westmoreland County, Pennsylvania at age 74.

Heinrich married **Anna Beitler**.

The child from this marriage was:

    46   i.   **Abraham Overholt**

93. Anna Beitler was born on 24 Mar 1745 in Bucks County, Pennsylvania and died on 5 Apr 1835 in Westmoreland County, Pennsylvania at age 90.

Anna married **Heinrich Oberholtzer**.

Eighth Generation (5th Great-Grandparents)

136. Joseph John Gilbert was born on 15 Jan 1675 in Little Leigh, Cheshire, England and died on 20 May 1765 in Byberry, Philadelphia, Pennsylvania at age 90.

Joseph married **Sarah James**.

The child from this marriage was:

    68   i.   **Benjamin Gilbert**

137. Sarah James was born on 1 Jul 1704 and died in 1789 at age 85.

Sarah married **Joseph John Gilbert**.

144. Thomas Howell, son of **John Howell** and **Sarah,** was born in 1699 in Powys, Wales.

Thomas married **Martha Williams**.

The child from this marriage was:

    72   i.   **John Howell**

145. Martha Williams was born about 1700 in Llangyniew, Powys, Wales and died after 1775.

Martha married **Thomas Howell**.

146. John Bevan Morgan was born in 1693 in Ystradgynlais, Breconshire, Wales and died on 22 Apr 1762 in Ystradgynlais, Breconshire, Wales at age 69.

John married **Catherine David** on 22 Feb 1717 in Ystradgynlais, Breconshire, Wales.

The child from this marriage was:

    73   i.   **Jenetta Catherine Morgan**

147. Catherine David was born in 1698 in Brecknock, Breconshire, Wales, died on 16 Dec 1743 in Brecknock, Breconshire, Wales at age 45, and was buried in Saint Michael Churchyard.

    Research Notes: Wallonia, Belgium Deaths, 1559-1984

Catherine married **John Bevan Morgan** on 22 Feb 1717 in Ystradgynlais, Breconshire, Wales.

152. Johannes H. Sauvage was born in 1698 and died in Feb 1761 in Berks County, Pennsylvania at age 63.

    Research Notes: Johannes H Sauvage arrived in America aboard the ship "Winter Galley" on May 9 1738 and settled in Berks County. He purchased the land where his graveyard is located on March 1743. He died in Feb 1761, signing his German will Johannass Sowas, an Americanized version of Sauvage. The name evolved to Sowash and later Soash as families moved west. Johannes was almost certainly buried in the graveyard on the property. The graveyard was vacated in 1865.

    There were two children named in his will: Heinrich and his sister Anna Elizabetha. Johnnes must have had another son as he had a grandson Joseph Savage who remained in Berks County and retained the "Sauvage/Savage" name. All other known descendants moved on to Westmoreland County, PA., and changed the name to Sowash or Soash.

    Information on Johannes Sauvage can be found at http://www.soash.org/soash.htm

    There have been many people copying information on Ancestry.com that has his parents as Jean and Jeanne (Peralt) Sauvage. I have researched the original records thoroughly and do not believe it to be accurate because:

    1) Jean & Jeanne Sauvage lived in Plelan Le Grand, Ille-et-Vilaine, Bretagne, France, on the northwestern coast. Because Johannes H Sauvage spoke German, he was probably born and lived in northeastern France (Alsace) or western Germany. Nearly all of the passengers on the immigration ship 'Winter Galley" were German from the Palatinate.

    2) Jean & Jeanne Sauvage were Catholic. From the time Johannes arrived in America, he was a member of the Reformed

Church. Brittany was not a safe place for Protestants after the Revocation of the Edict of Nantes in 1685.

3) I checked out the records in Plelan Le Grand, and there are no birth records for Johannes in 1698. They had a son Jan, born 16th October, 1700. There is no marriage record where he married Susanna. Jean and Jeanne were married 15th July 1698.

The only source for Johannes H. Sauvage's birth year is the passenger list which lists him as age 40 upon his arrival in Philadelphia in 1738.

It seems someone just found a Jean Sauvage in France out of thousands and made this erroneous connection.

Johannes married **Susanna**.

Children from this marriage were:

76	i.	**Henry Sowash**
	ii.	**Anna Elizabetha Sauvage**

153. Susanna.

Susanna married **Johannes H. Sauvage**.

160. Abraham Leasure was born on 11 Apr 1695 in Switzerland, was christened on 13 Apr 1695, and died in 1785 in Westmoreland County, Pennsylvania at age 90.

Research Notes: About Abraham Leasure, I Rev. War Vet.
THE FOLLOWING INFORMATION WAS FURNISHED BY PHIL LASHER:
Abraham's dates are b. 1695 d. 1785 in Bedford County. Some accounts have him living as late as 1790 but all have him as died in Bedford County. Also most Rev soldiers filed for a pension between 1785 and 1790 but Abraham did not.

The government veterans grave locator lists only two Leasure's in Unity cemetery (both Abraham b. 1713 d. 1803 & brother Georgeb. 1728 d. 1809 attached.) Abraham b. 1713 d. 1803 and his wife Margaret b. 1715 d. 1818 both died and were buried on their farm Westmoreland County, near the present site of the Westmoreland county fair grounds. Their bodies were moved at a later date to the unity cemetery, and buried next to his brother George.

The government veterans grave locator lists only two Leasure's in Unity cemetery (both Abraham b. 1713 d. 1803 & brother Georgeb. 1728 d. 1809 attached.) Abraham b. 1713 d. 1803 and his wife Margaret b. 1715 d. 1818 both died and were buried on their farm Westmoreland County, near the present site of the Westmoreland county fair grounds. Their bodies were moved at a later date to the unity cemetery, and buried next to his brother George.

I am still looking for Abrahams records at the national archives and if they are ever found I will let you know where he is buried but we can be sure it is not in Unity cemetery.

Note: Abraham came from Novarri, France in 1754. He was a French Huguenot. Abraham was married to Margarette. The original spelling of his name was LeSouer or LeSueur

We can show that all his sons served in the same unit from Upper Dauphin Co., Pa., as did he in the Revolution. All his sons received their Revolutionary War bounty property in Westmoreland County except for Benjamin who became Lasher. The Westmoreland property can be traced to the bounty property given to the vary unit from Upper Dauphin Co., Pa., that they all served in.

Rev. A. Stapleton one of the first pastors in Westmoreland county wrote:

BIOGRAPHY: Rev. A. Stapleton, in his memorial of the Huguenots in America, gives the following concerning the Leasure family: "The Leasure family is both ancient and honorable, and was originally seated in the Province of Navarre, France. At the Revocation a branch of this family was compelled to flee to Switzerland for safety, and from whence came Abraham Leasure, who arrived in America in 1754, and located in upper Dauphin County, Pa., where the family name is still extant. A son of the immigrant located in Westmoreland County, Pa., where his descendants became prominent, notably Gen. Daniel Leasure, a distinguished officer of the Civil War ." (Stewart's History)

Thanks Phil Lasher

Father: Pierre LESUEUR b: ABT 1669 in Switzerland Mother: Jeanne DROUOT b: ABT 1671 in Basel, Switzerland

Marriage 1 MARGARETTE b: ABT 1691 in France Married: 1713 Children Has No Children Abraham LEASURE b: BET 1712 AND 1713 in Basel, Switzerland Has No Children Peter LEASURE b: ABT 1719 in Basel, Switzerland Has No Children Margaret LEASURE b: ABT 1725 in Basel, Switzerland Has Children George LEASURE b: 3 NOV 1728 in Basel, Switzerland Has No Children John LEASURE b: 1731 in Basel, Switzerland

There is much confusion and controversy both in regard to the place of Abrahams birth (Ancestry; Neatherlands, others France and findagrave; Switzerland) and, secondly, his father (Ancestry; Abraham, Our Family; Pierre, My Heritage; Jean Francois)

Abraham married **Margarette Poinsett**.

The child from this marriage was:

> 80   i.   **Abraham Leasure**

161. Margarette Poinsett was born in 1691 in France and died in Westmoreland County, Pennsylvania.

Margarette married **Abraham Leasure**.

176. Matthias Tintsman/Dinstman was born about 1726 in Germany.

Matthias married **Aylse**.

The child from this marriage was:

> 88   i.   **Adam Tintsman/Dinstman**

177. Aylse.

Aylse married **Matthias Tintsman/Dinstman**.

184. Martin Oberholtzer was born in 1709 in Frankfurt-am-Main, Heiliges Römisches Reich Deutscher Nation and died on 5 Nov 1744 in Deep Run, Bedminster Township, Bucks County, Pennsylvania at age 35.

Research Notes: Martin Overholt, born in the Rhenish Palatinate in 1709, was one of the thousands who were compelled by religious persecutions and the virulence of Franco-German warfare to forsake their native land in the

early part of the 18th century. The exact date of his arrival is not known, but it must have occurred soon after his majority in 1730. That he accompanied his fellow refugees to the recognized meeting place, at Germantown, may be safely assumed. But presently he passed on to Bucks County on the Delaware, acquired a farm apparently by lease, in Bedminster Township, married in 1736, died in 1744, in his 36th year, and was buried in the Mennonite Graveyard, leaving a son, Henry, born in 1739.

682. Martin Oberholtzer, born 1709 in Germany; died April 05, 1744. He married 683. Agnes Kolb November 02, 1736.

683. Agnes Kolb, born April 18, 1713; died February 02, 1786. She was the daughter of 1366. Henry Kolb and 1367. Barbara ? Fretz.

Children of Martin Oberholtzer and Agnes Kolb are:

i. Martin Oberholtzer

ii. John Oberholtzer

iii. Maria Oberholtzer

341 iv. Barbara Oberholtzer, born November 20, 1737; died May 08, 1823 in Bedminster, Bucks Co., PA; married Christian Fretz 1757.

v. Henry Oberholtzer, born February 05, 1738/39; died December 05, 1813; married Anna Butler January 03, 1765.

Lots of good information about the Overholts in Germany here:
http://www.karensbranches.com/OberholtzerSites/Germany.html

NOTE: The discussion below credited to Betty May contains information culled from the 1903 work of Rev. A.J. Fretz titled "A Genealogical Record of the Descendants of Martin Oberholtzer: Together with Historical and Biographical Sketches and Illustrated with Portraits and Other Illustrations." (Milton, N.J.: The Press of Evergreen News, 1903).

Please also note that the Martin in the top paragraph of the the information below is the father of the Martin Jr in the second paragraph below. It is thought that Martin Sr's headstone (shown here) is a modern replacement for an earlier stone where the name of "Oberholtzer" was used (the surname being changed to the more commonly used and 'Americanized' version for various reasons). The discussion of Martin Jr outlines reasons for this change. ~ Updated by Carl Christensen October 2011.

Martin Oberholtzer (Overholt) Date of Birth 1709 at Frankfort-on-the-main (Now known as Frankfort) Germany. Married Agnes (Maiden Name unknown) on November 2, 1736. She was born April 18, 1713. They were married only eight years and had five children before his death on April 5, 1744 One child died in infancy. The four remaining children were: Barbara, Henry, Marie and Martin Jr. Agnes married a second time to William Nash and was his third wife. They had four more children. He died in 1760. Agnes died February 15, 1786 and is buried in the same cemetery where Martin is buried. Deep Run Mennonite Cemetery East.

Martin Oberholtzer Jr. and other family members changed their last name to the more English version of the name, Overholt. He was born December 20, 1743 in Bucks Co., PA. He married Esther Fretz in 1770. She was the daughter of Christian Fretz who had come to this country around 1720 along with two brothers from Baden, Germany. Martin and Esther had four children by the time the Revolutionary War broke out and fled to Canada for protection. They did not like the cold winters in Canada and moved back to Bucks Co. PA when the war was over. In 1810 Martin traveled to Ohio and purchased land in Coshocton and Tuscarawas Countied intending to move his large family (He now had forteen children) to Ohio. About six weeks before they were to make the move, he bled to death from a cancer on the neck. Esther took her large family and moved to Tuscarawas Co. Ohio.

Information supplied by Betty May (Overholt descendent)

Martin Oberholtzer's father was Marcus "Mark" Oberholtzer of 1664 to 1726.

Children of Martin Oberholtzer ("senior") are: Barbara Heinrich (aka Henry)- see link below Maria John Martin, Jr

Aug 30, 2016 7:41 PM - Findagrave User #47484531 claims that Martin's birth date is April 5, 1709 but provides no source for this information.

NOTE: That while the general area that Martin is to have emigrated from is now known as Germany, in the early 1700s, it was still a hodgepodge of Principalities that did not always have a common government. So noting his birth as 'Germany' is problematic.
See Deep Run East Mennonite East Cemetery notes about the differences between each cemetery at 'Deep Run'

Martin married **Agnes Fretz**.

The child from this marriage was:

    92   i.   **Heinrich Oberholtzer**

185. Agnes Fretz was born in 1713 and died in 1788 at age 75.

Agnes married **Martin Oberholtzer**.

Ninth Generation (6th Great-Grandparents)

288. John Howell, son of **Thomas Howell** and **Alice Powell,** was born in 1679 in Oswestry, Shropshire, England and died in 1761 in Oswestry, Shropshire, England at age 82.

John married **Sarah**.

The child from this marriage was:

    144   i.   **Thomas Howell**

289. Sarah was born in 1667 and died in 1729 at age 62.

Sarah married **John Howell**.

Tenth Generation (7th Great-Grandparents)

576. Thomas Howell was born in 1650 in Sweeney and died in 1717 in Oswestry, Shropshire, , England at age 67.

Thomas married **Alice Powell** on 20 Jul 1678 in Oswestry, Shropshire, England.

The child from this marriage was:

    288   i.   **John Howell**

577. Alice Powell was born in 1659 in Treflach, Shropshire, England and died about 1696 about age 37.

Alice married **Thomas Howell** on 20 Jul 1678 in Oswestry, Shropshire, England.

Chart no. 1

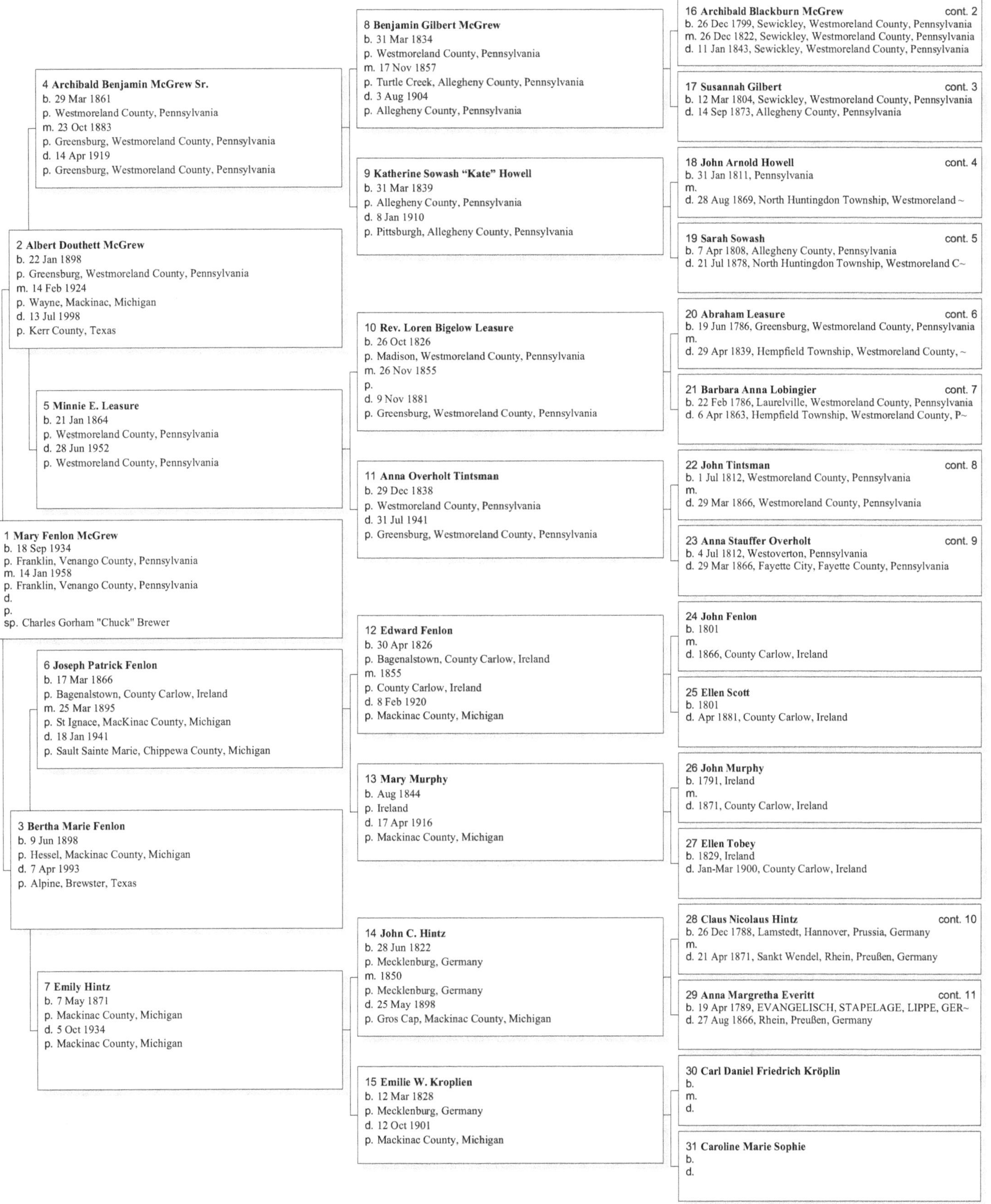

Produced by: Tennessee Research Company on 5 Sep 2019

Pedigree Chart for Archibald Blackburn McGrew

No. 1 on this chart is the same as no. 16 on chart no. 1

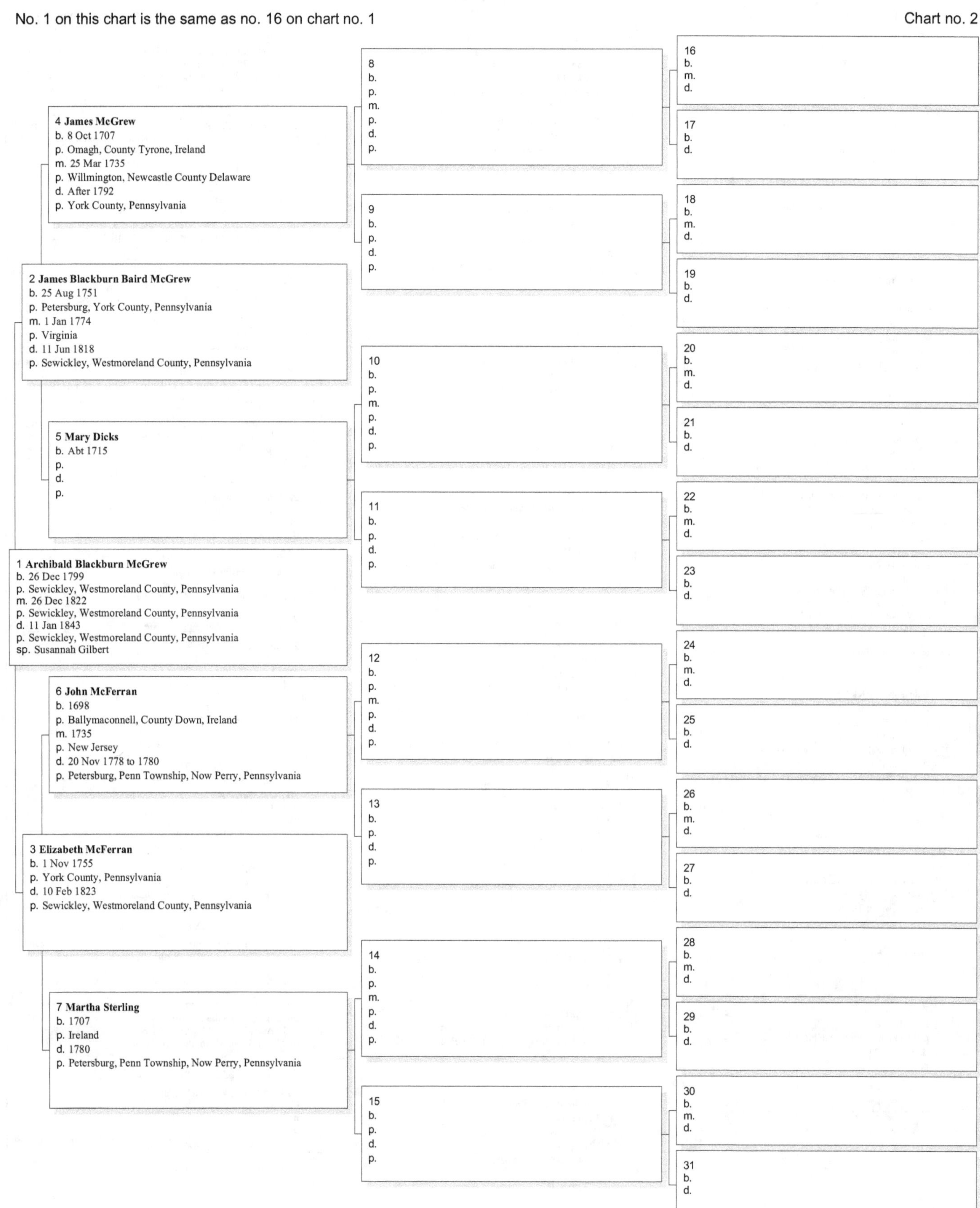

No. 1 on this chart is the same as no. 17 on chart no. 1

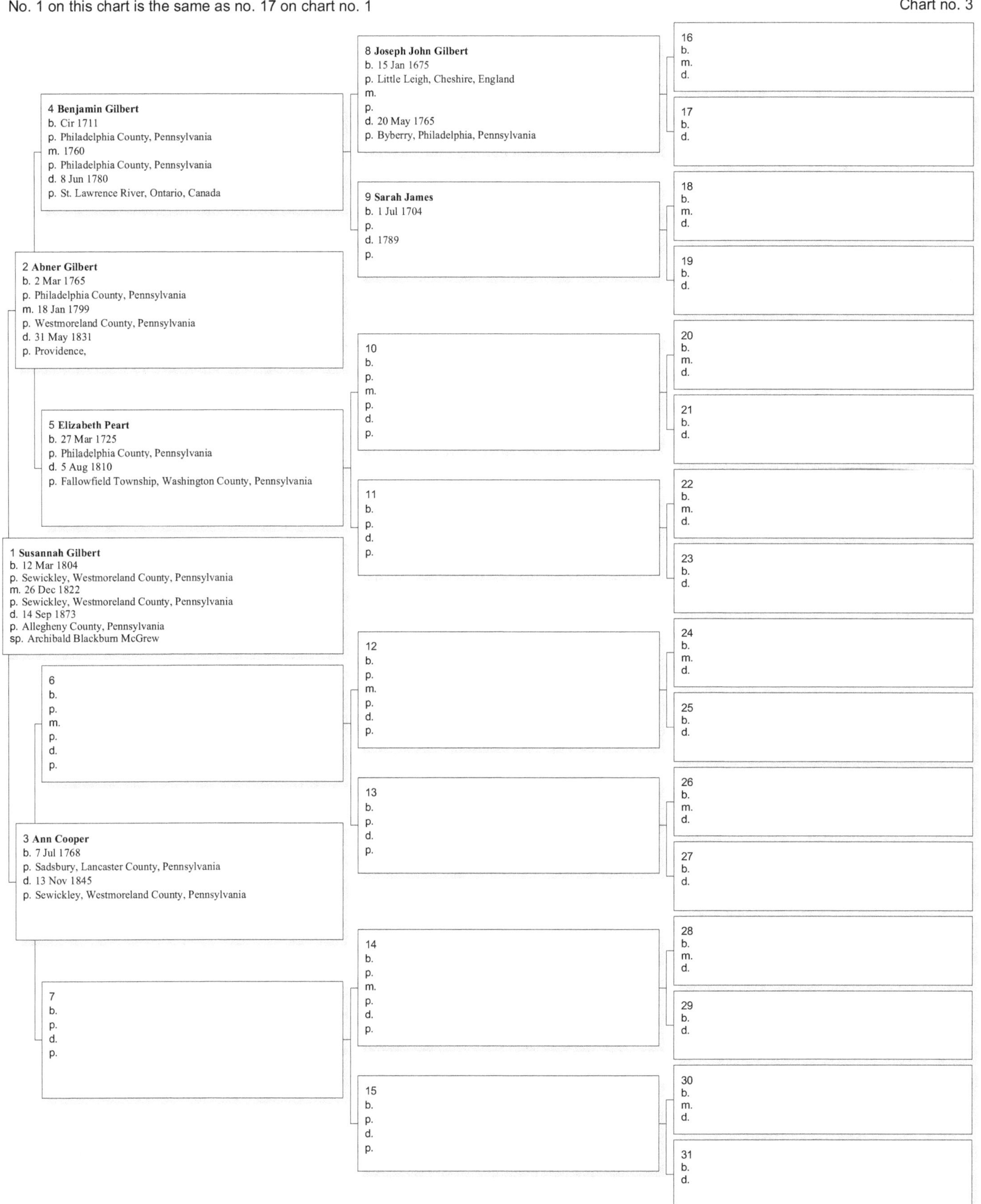

Pedigree Chart for John Arnold Howell

No. 1 on this chart is the same as no. 18 on chart no. 1

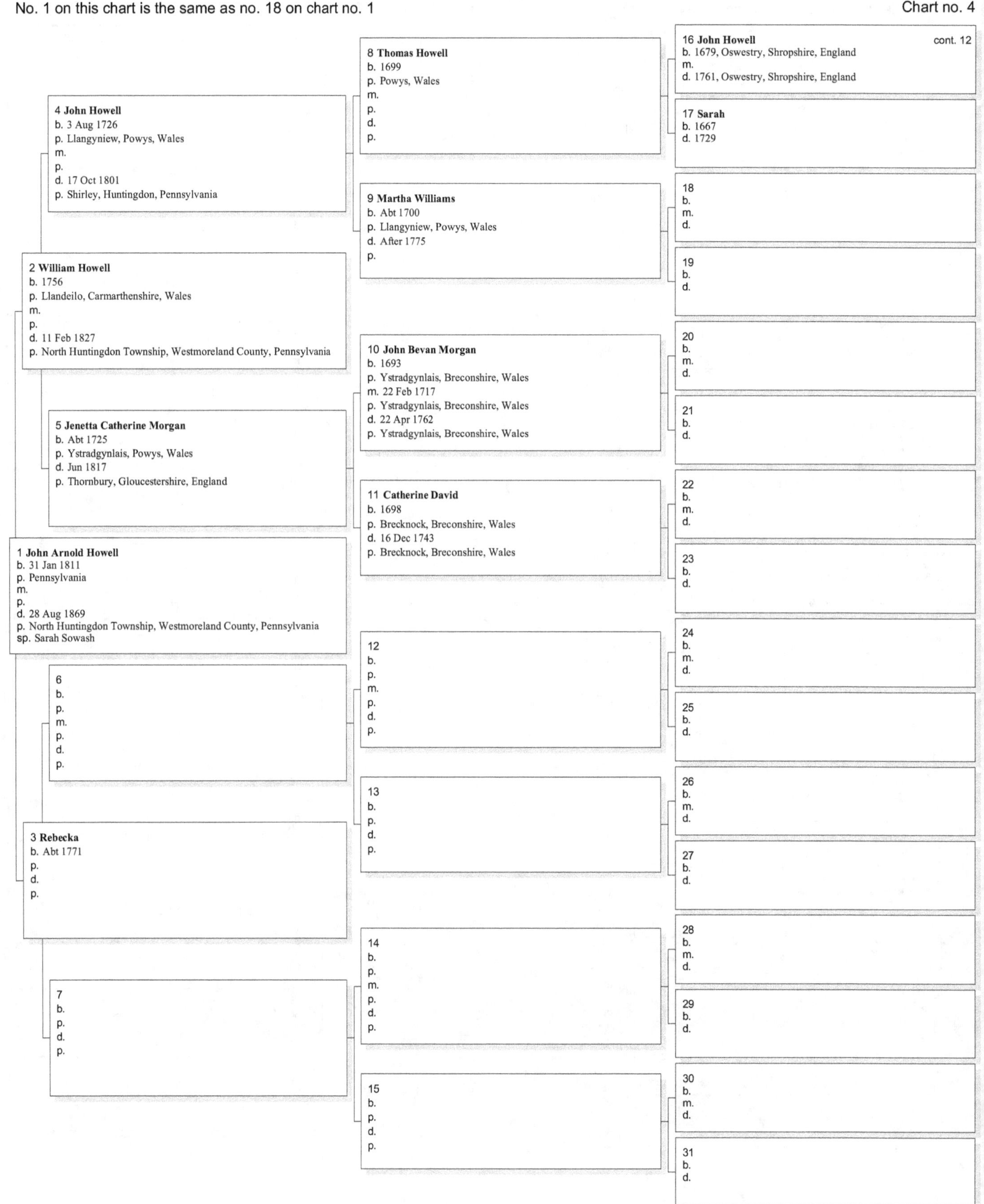

4 John Howell
b. 3 Aug 1726
p. Llangyniew, Powys, Wales
m.
p.
d. 17 Oct 1801
p. Shirley, Huntingdon, Pennsylvania

2 William Howell
b. 1756
p. Llandeilo, Carmarthenshire, Wales
m.
p.
d. 11 Feb 1827
p. North Huntingdon Township, Westmoreland County, Pennsylvania

5 Jenetta Catherine Morgan
b. Abt 1725
p. Ystradgynlais, Powys, Wales
d. Jun 1817
p. Thornbury, Gloucestershire, England

1 John Arnold Howell
b. 31 Jan 1811
p. Pennsylvania
m.
p.
d. 28 Aug 1869
p. North Huntingdon Township, Westmoreland County, Pennsylvania
sp. Sarah Sowash

6
b.
p.
m.
p.
d.
p.

3 Rebecka
b. Abt 1771
p.
d.
p.

7
b.
p.
d.
p.

8 Thomas Howell
b. 1699
p. Powys, Wales
m.
p.
d.
p.

9 Martha Williams
b. Abt 1700
p. Llangyniew, Powys, Wales
d. After 1775
p.

10 John Bevan Morgan
b. 1693
p. Ystradgynlais, Breconshire, Wales
m. 22 Feb 1717
p. Ystradgynlais, Breconshire, Wales
d. 22 Apr 1762
p. Ystradgynlais, Breconshire, Wales

11 Catherine David
b. 1698
p. Brecknock, Breconshire, Wales
d. 16 Dec 1743
p. Brecknock, Breconshire, Wales

12
b.
p.
m.
p.
d.
p.

13
b.
p.
d.
p.

14
b.
p.
m.
p.
d.
p.

15
b.
p.
d.
p.

16 John Howell   cont. 12
b. 1679, Oswestry, Shropshire, England
m.
d. 1761, Oswestry, Shropshire, England

17 Sarah
b. 1667
d. 1729

18
b.
m.
d.

19
b.
d.

20
b.
m.
d.

21
b.
d.

22
b.
m.
d.

23
b.
d.

24
b.
m.
d.

25
b.
d.

26
b.
m.
d.

27
b.
d.

28
b.
m.
d.

29
b.
d.

30
b.
m.
d.

31
b.
d.

No. 1 on this chart is the same as no. 19 on chart no. 1

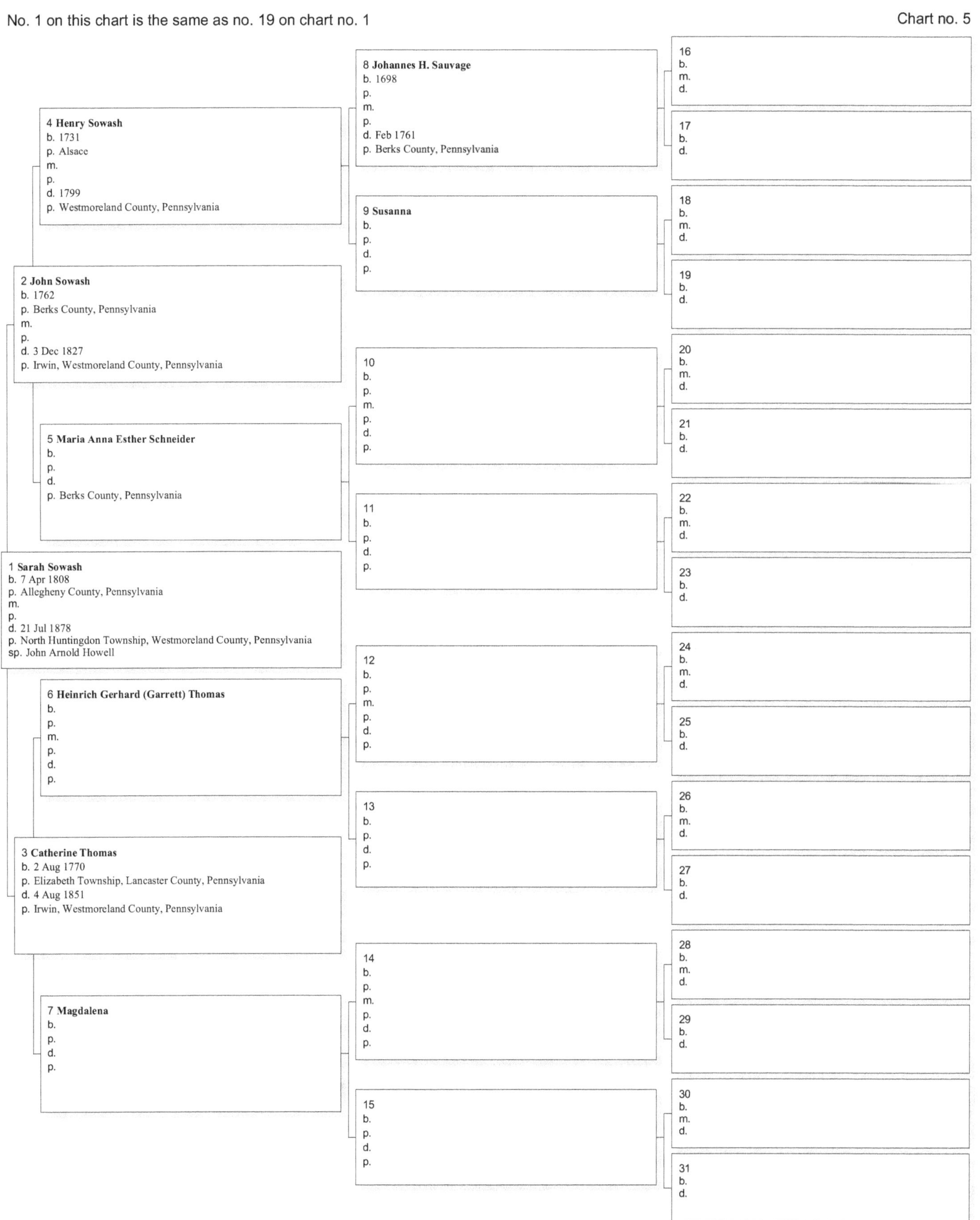

No. 1 on this chart is the same as no. 20 on chart no. 1

Chart no. 6

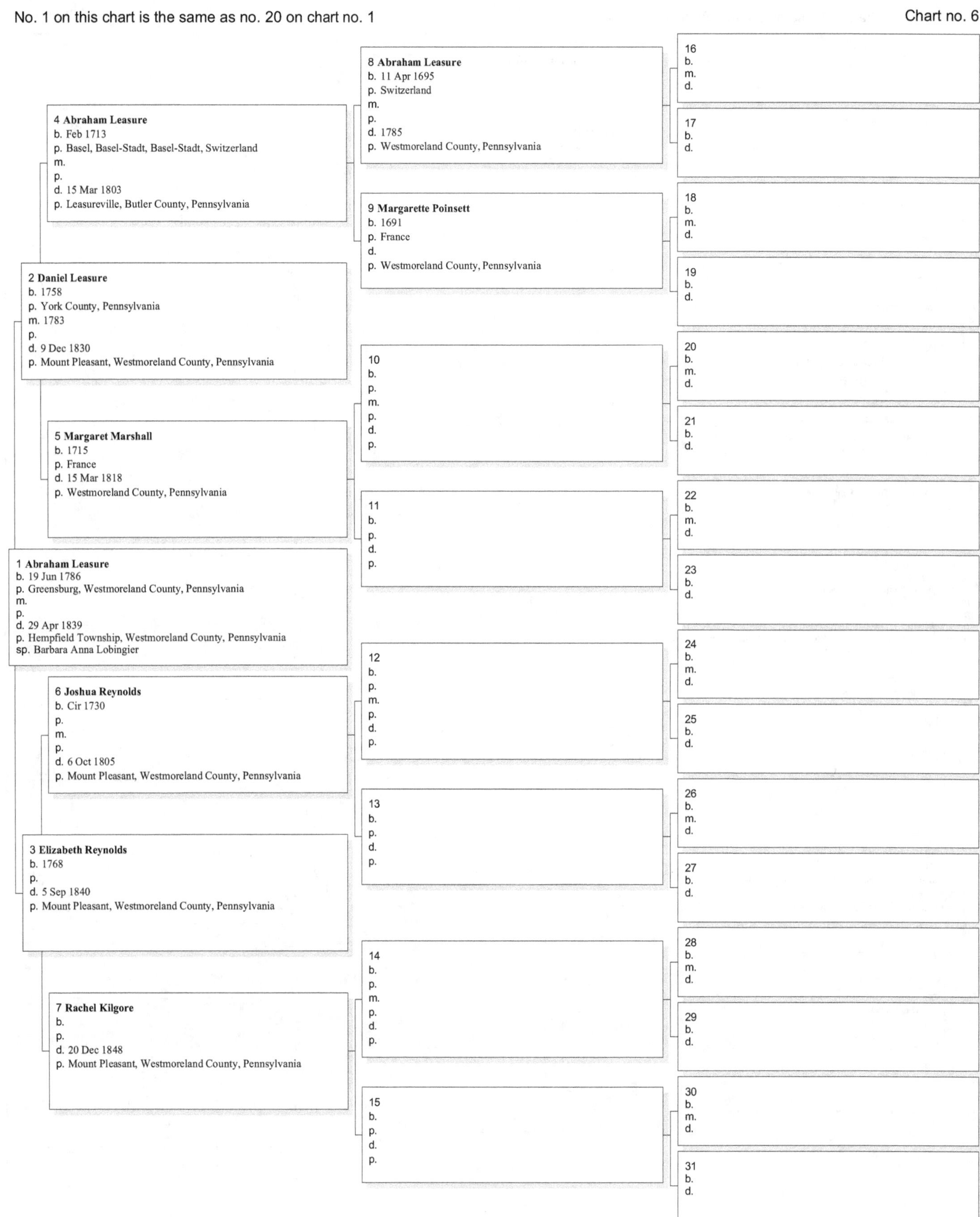

No. 1 on this chart is the same as no. 21 on chart no. 1

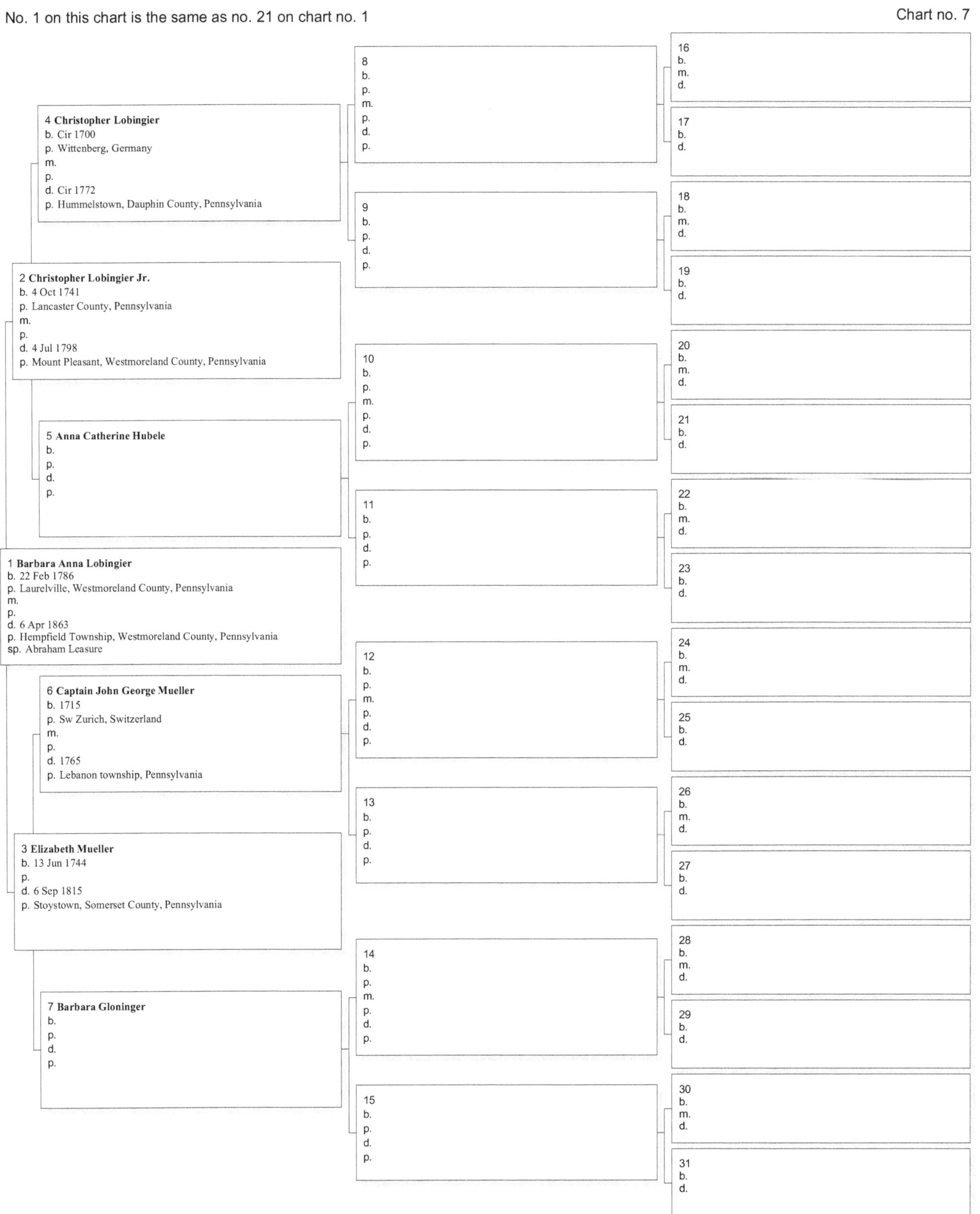

Pedigree Chart for John Tintsman

No. 1 on this chart is the same as no. 22 on chart no. 1

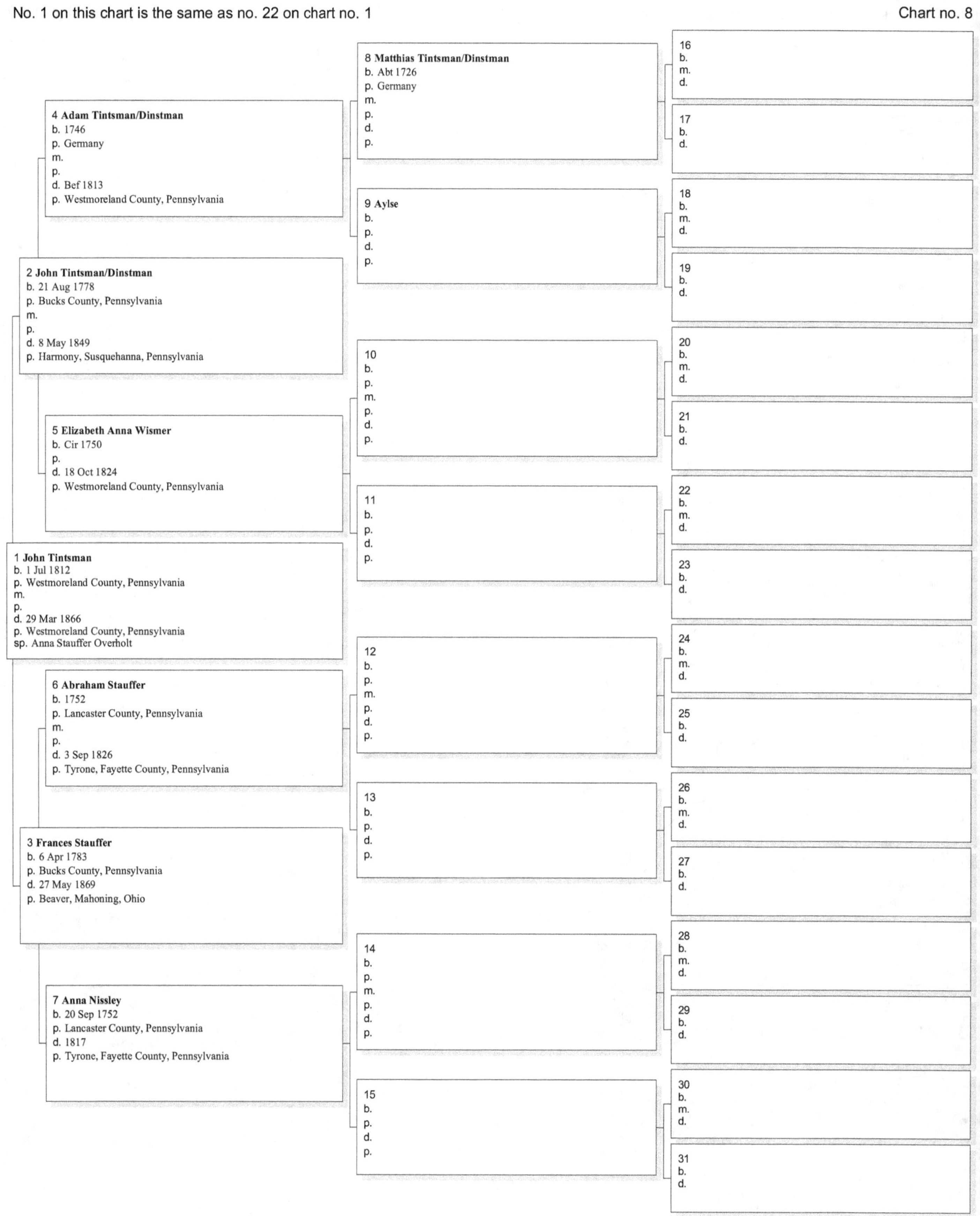

No. 1 on this chart is the same as no. 23 on chart no. 1

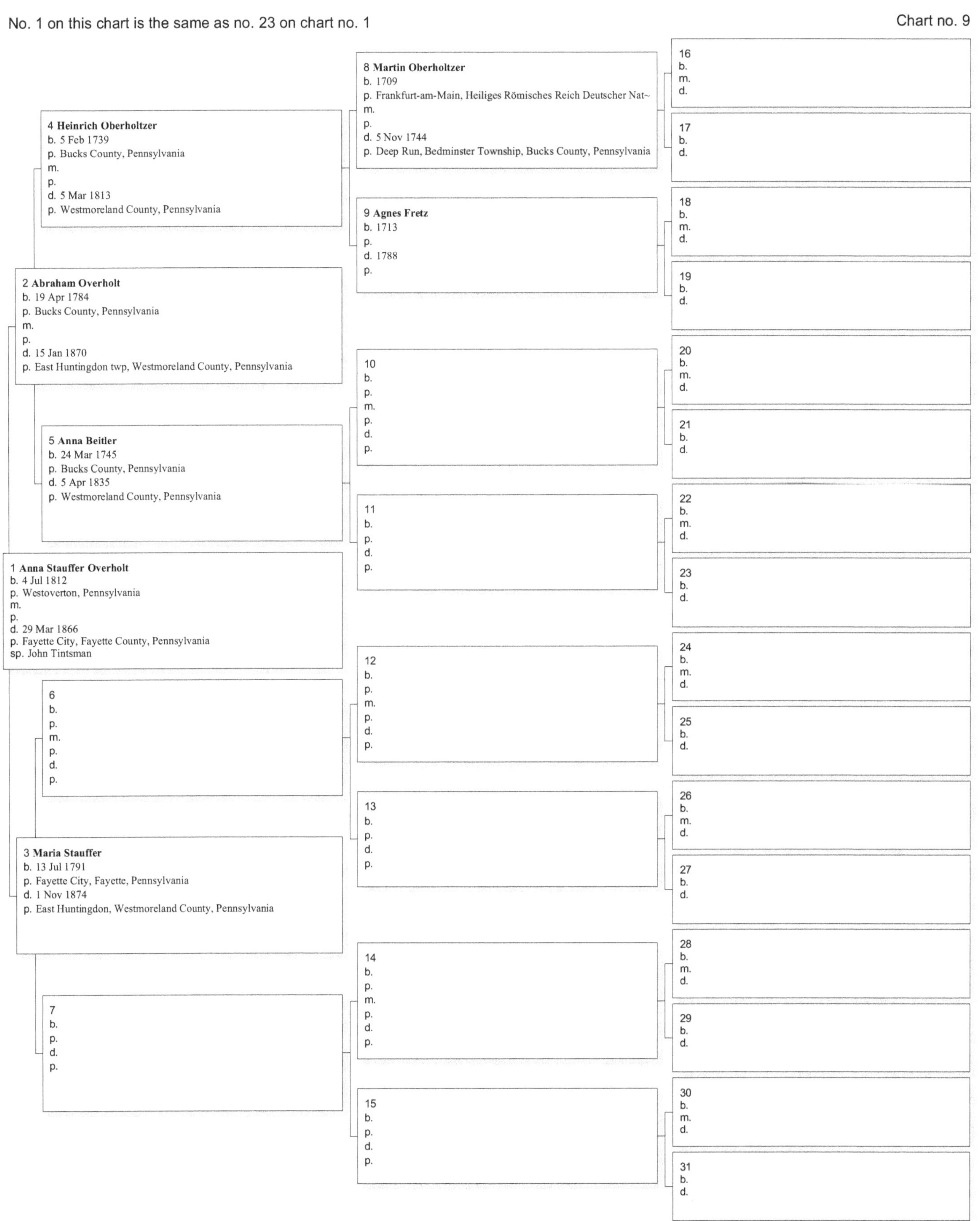

4 Heinrich Oberholtzer
b. 5 Feb 1739
p. Bucks County, Pennsylvania
m.
p.
d. 5 Mar 1813
p. Westmoreland County, Pennsylvania

2 Abraham Overholt
b. 19 Apr 1784
p. Bucks County, Pennsylvania
m.
p.
d. 15 Jan 1870
p. East Huntingdon twp, Westmoreland County, Pennsylvania

5 Anna Beitler
b. 24 Mar 1745
p. Bucks County, Pennsylvania
d. 5 Apr 1835
p. Westmoreland County, Pennsylvania

1 Anna Stauffer Overholt
b. 4 Jul 1812
p. Westoverton, Pennsylvania
m.
p.
d. 29 Mar 1866
p. Fayette City, Fayette County, Pennsylvania
sp. John Tintsman

6
b.
p.
m.
p.
d.
p.

3 Maria Stauffer
b. 13 Jul 1791
p. Fayette City, Fayette, Pennsylvania
d. 1 Nov 1874
p. East Huntingdon, Westmoreland County, Pennsylvania

7
b.
p.
d.
p.

8 Martin Oberholtzer
b. 1709
p. Frankfurt-am-Main, Heiliges Römisches Reich Deutscher Nat~
m.
p.
d. 5 Nov 1744
p. Deep Run, Bedminster Township, Bucks County, Pennsylvania

9 Agnes Fretz
b. 1713
p.
d. 1788
p.

10
b.
p.
m.
p.
d.
p.

11
b.
p.
d.
p.

12
b.
p.
m.
p.
d.
p.

13
b.
p.
d.
p.

14
b.
p.
m.
p.
d.
p.

15
b.
p.
d.
p.

16
b.
m.
d.

17
b.
d.

18
b.
m.
d.

19
b.
d.

20
b.
m.
d.

21
b.
d.

22
b.
m.
d.

23
b.
d.

24
b.
m.
d.

25
b.
d.

26
b.
m.
d.

27
b.
d.

28
b.
m.
d.

29
b.
d.

30
b.
m.
d.

31
b.
d.

No. 1 on this chart is the same as no. 28 on chart no. 1

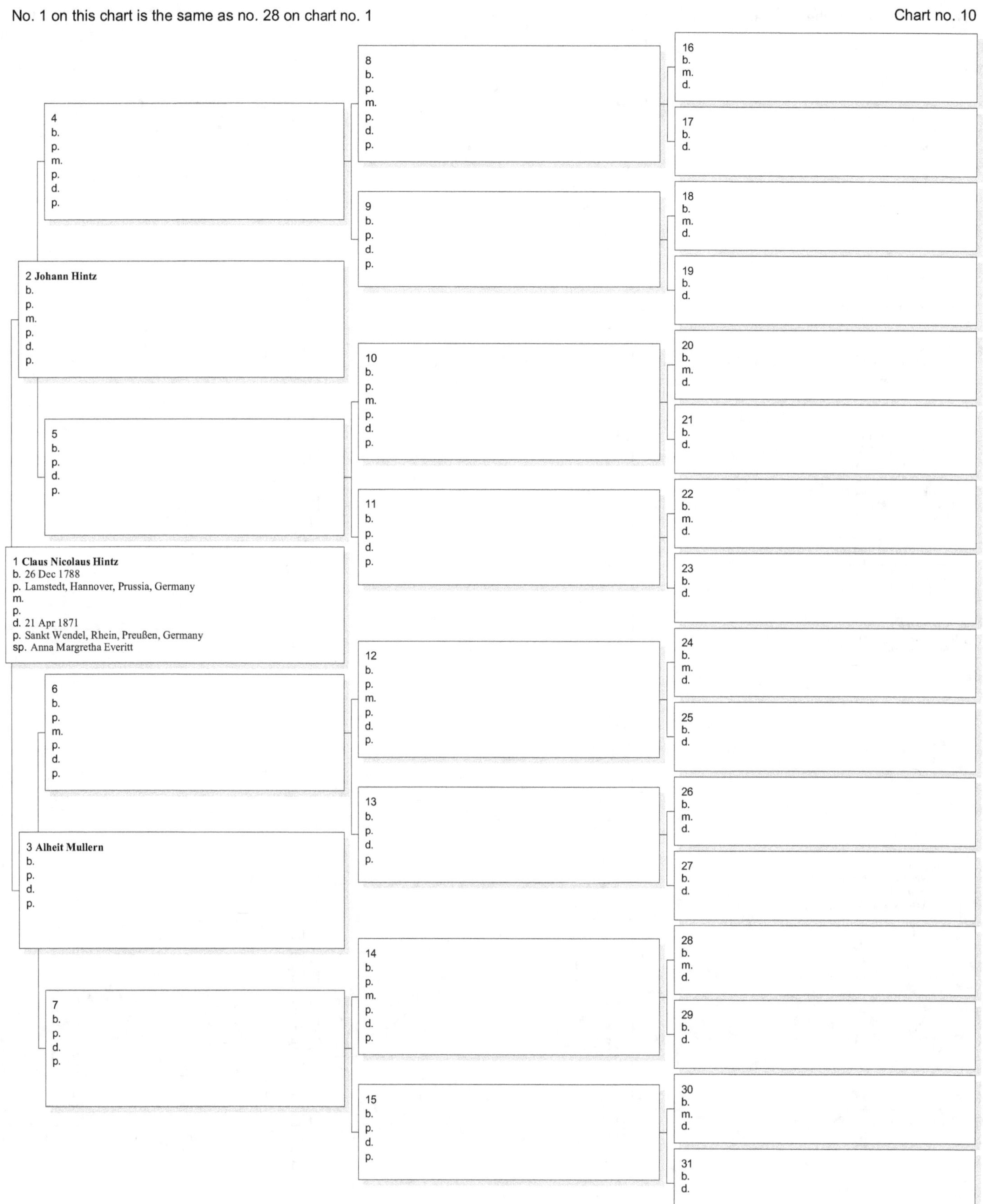

No. 1 on this chart is the same as no. 29 on chart no. 1

1 **Anna Margretha Everitt**
b. 19 Apr 1789
p. EVANGELISCH, STAPELAGE, LIPPE, GERMANY
m.
p.
d. 27 Aug 1866
p. Rhein, Preußen, Germany
sp. Claus Nicolaus Hintz

2 **Johann Hermann Everitt**
b.
p.
m.
p.
d.
p.

3 **Anna Margretha Everts**
b.
p.
d.
p.

4
b.
p.
m.
p.
d.
p.

5
b.
p.
d.
p.

6
b.
p.
m.
p.
d.
p.

7
b.
p.
d.
p.

8
b.
p.
m.
p.
d.
p.

9
b.
p.
d.
p.

10
b.
p.
m.
p.
d.
p.

11
b.
p.
d.
p.

12
b.
p.
m.
p.
d.
p.

13
b.
p.
d.
p.

14
b.
p.
m.
p.
d.
p.

15
b.
p.
d.
p.

16
b.
m.
d.

17
b.
d.

18
b.
m.
d.

19
b.
d.

20
b.
m.
d.

21
b.
d.

22
b.
m.
d.

23
b.
d.

24
b.
m.
d.

25
b.
d.

26
b.
m.
d.

27
b.
d.

28
b.
m.
d.

29
b.
d.

30
b.
m.
d.

31
b.
d.

No. 1 on this chart is the same as no. 16 on chart no. 4

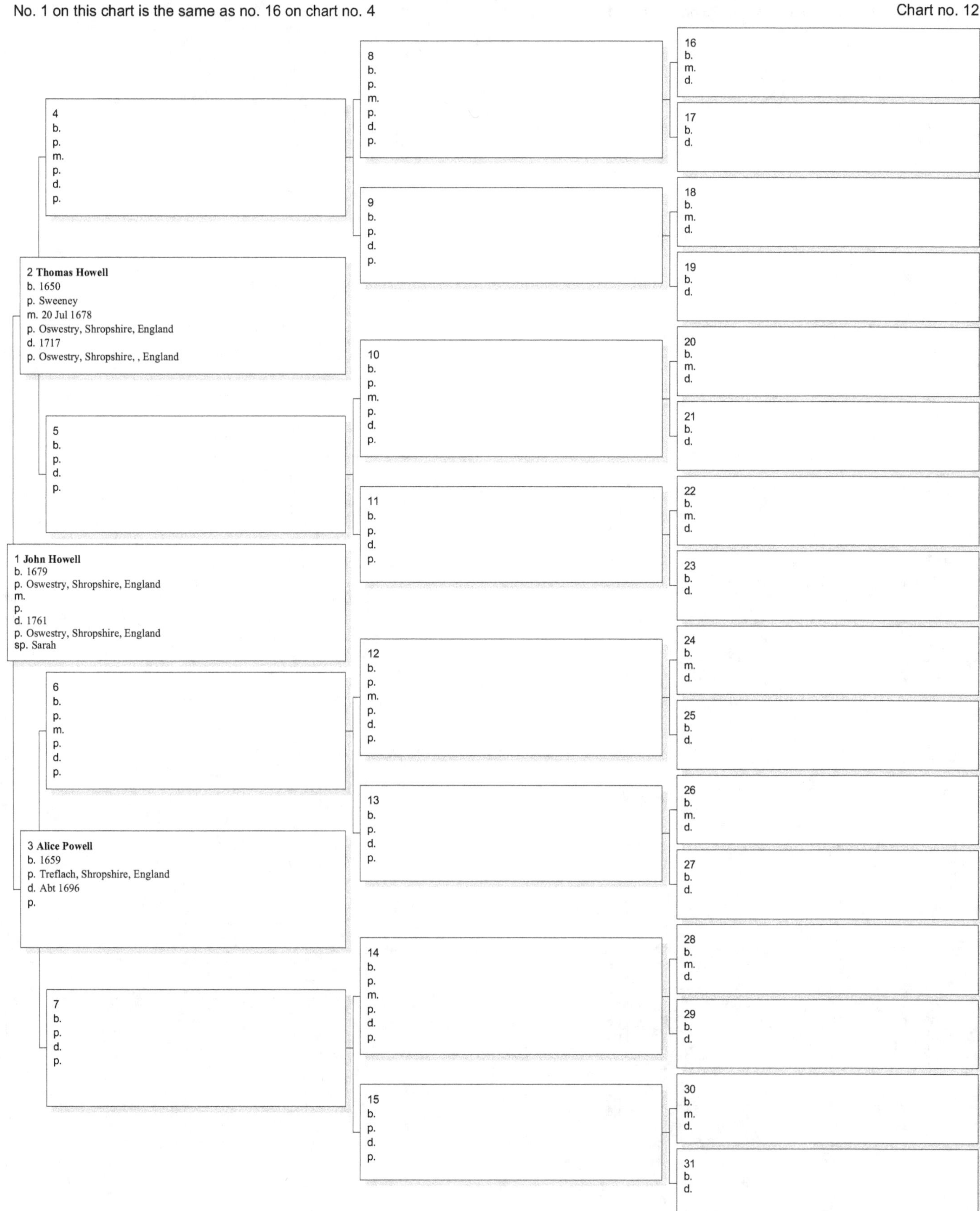

First Generation

1. James McGrew was born on 8 Oct 1707 in Omagh, County Tyrone, Ireland and died after 1792 in York County, Pennsylvania.

Research Notes: James McGrew was born about 1707 to Robert McGrew and his wife, Isabella.

He married Mary Dicks on Mar. 25, 1735 at Holy Trinity (Old Swedes) Church in Wilmington, Delaware.[1]

James was assessed in London Grove, Chester County, Pennsylvania in 1729 and 1734.

James and his wife brought a certificate from Hopewell, Virginia to Warrington Monthly Meeting in 1750.[2]

The births of their children were recorded at the Menallen Monthly Meeting.[3]

Children

Finley b. 1st mo. [Mar] 13, 1735, m. Dinah Cox; and removed about 1787 to the Redstone region of Pennsylvania
Deborah b. 7th mo. [Sep] 14, 1739 m. Joseph Blackburn in 1758
Ann b. 4th mo. [Jun] 29, 1741, m. Elijah Newlin
Nathan, b. 3rd mo. [May] 10 1743, d. 1769 m. Rachel Blackburn in 1767
Simeon b. 11th mo. [Jan] 5, 1745/6, m. Martha McKnight
Mary b. 11th mo. [Jan] 5 1748/9, m. Moses Blackburn in 1767
James b. 6th mo. [Aug] 25 1751 m. Elizabeth McFerran about 1774 and removed to the Redstone region about 1794

Holy Trinity (Old Swedes) Church in Wilmington, Delaware

The Will of James McGrew filed in York County, Pennsylvania

In the name of God Amen I James McGrew of Menallin Township in the County of York and State of Pennsylvania, being weak in Body but of Perfect mind and Memory, blessed be Almighty God for the same calling to mind the mortality of Body and that it is appointed for all men once to die, do make and Publish this my last will and Testament in the manner and form following that is to say principally and first of all give and Recommend my soul to Almighty God who gave it, and my body to the earth to be buried in a decent and Christian manner at discretion of my Executors as will be hereafter named and as touching such worldly Estate wherewith it pleased God to bless me with in this life I give and dispose of the same in the following manner viz first,

I order that all my just debts and funeral expenses be discharged and paid. Then I give and bequeath unto my youngest son James McGrew all my real estate in Lands lying and being in Menallen Township, York County and State aforesaid on which I am now living to him his heirs, Executors, Administrators and Assigns forever.

Also I give and bequeath to my said son James two chairs and one table, and griddle and pair of Stilyards and a frying pan also all the farming utensils that belongs to the said farm.

I also allow my son James McGrew to pay the sum of Forty Pounds to my son Simeon McGrew to be paid out of my real estate to be paid in Gold or Silver to be paid in Eighteen months after my decease.

Also I give and bequeath to my well beloved son Simeon McGrew the sum of Forty Pounds in Gold or Silver also my fine hat and Saddle which is to be paid out of my Personal Estate and to be paid Eighteen months after my Decease, this shall be his full share and no more being in part already advanced.

Also I give and bequeath to my beloved son Finley McGrew the sum of three Pounds in Gold or Silver (I also allow my son Finley my Riding rein and greatcoat and strait bodied coat) to be paid out of the Personal Estate to be paid in Eighteen months after my Decease. This shall be his full share and no more being in part already advanced.

Also I give and bequeath to my well beloved Daughter Deborah Blackburn, wife of Joseph Blackburn, deceased, the Sum of Twenty Pounds in Gold or Silver to be paid Eighteen months after my Decease, exclusive of what she has already received.

Descendants of James McGrew

Also I give and bequeath to my Granddaughter Mary Brandon, the sum of three Pounds in Gold or Silver to be paid out of my Personal Estate Eighteen months after my Decease.

Also I give and bequeath to my three daughters, viz, Deborah, Ann and Mary all the remainder of my personal estate after the legacies already mentioned to be divided equally between the three.

Also I give and bequeath to Sarah Kelsey wife of Joseph Kelsey my bed and bedding.

Also I give and bequeath to my Grand Daughter Jean McGrew, daughter of James McGrew one case of Drawers.

And lastly I do constitute and appoint my aforesaid son James McGrew and my nephew Alexander McGrew my whole and Sole Executors to see the orderly accomplishments of this my last will and Testament according to the true intent and meaning thereof also to pay and settle all said Legacies in Eighteen months after my decease. In confirmation whereof I have hereunto set my Hand and Seal this Nineteenth Day of December in the year of our Lord one thousand seven hundred and ninety two, 1792.

James McGrew (X His Mark)

Signed, Sealed and Pronounced and Declared as my Last will and testament in presence of Archibald McGrew, Wm. McGrew

Sources Records of Holy Trinity (Old Swedes) Church, Wilmington, Del., from 1697 to 1773; pg. 359.
? Immigration of the Irish Quakers into Pennsylvania in York County, Established in 1747 from Sadsbury. "James McGrew, kinsman doubtless of Finley McGrew, brought a certificate for himself and wife from Hopewell, Va to Warrington Monthly Meeting in 1750. A James Magrew probably the same, was assessed in London Grove, Chester County in 1729 and 1734. Children of James and Mary McGrew; Finley b. Jan 13, 1736, m. Dinah Cox; and removed about 1787 to the Redstone region of Pennsylvania; Deborah b. Jul 14, 1739 m. Joseph Blackburn in 1758; Ann b. Apr 29, 1741, m. ? Newlin; Nathan, B. Mar 10 1743, d. 1769 m. Rachel Blackburn in 1767; Simon b. Nov 5, 1745, Mary b. Nov 5 1748, m. Moses Blackburn in 1767, James b. Jun 25 1751 m. Elizabeth McFerran, (p381) about 1774 and removed to the Redstone region about 1794. Children of James and Elizabeth McFerran McGrew; Mary b. May 10 1774, m. Joel Hutton; Nathan m. Elizabeth Winder; Jane; James B. Deborah m. Samuel McGrew; Joseph; Simon; Finley; Thomas; John B; Jacob; Archibald m. Susanna Gilbert.
? Swarthmore College; Swarthmore, Pennsylvania; Minutes and Deaths 1785-1884; Collection: Baltimore Yearly Meeting Minutes; Call Number: RG2/B/M461 3.1; Menallen Monthly Meeting; Minutes and Deaths 1785-1884; pg. 35.

James married **Mary Dicks** on 25 Mar 1735 in Willmington, Newcastle County Delaware. Mary was born about 1715.

The child from this marriage was:

+ 2 M   i.   **James Blackburn Baird McGrew** was born on 25 Aug 1751 in Petersburg, York County, Pennsylvania, died on 11 Jun 1818 in Sewickley, Westmoreland County, Pennsylvania at age 66, and was buried in Friends Burial Ground.

Second Generation (Children)

2. James Blackburn Baird McGrew *(James [1])* was born on 25 Aug 1751 in Petersburg, York County, Pennsylvania, died on 11 Jun 1818 in Sewickley, Westmoreland County, Pennsylvania at age 66, and was buried in Friends Burial Ground.

James married **Elizabeth McFerran,** daughter of **John McFerran** and **Martha Sterling,** on 1 Jan 1774 in Virginia. Elizabeth was born on 1 Nov 1755 in York County, Pennsylvania and died on 10 Feb 1823 in Sewickley, Westmoreland County, Pennsylvania at age 67.

Children from this marriage were:

3 M   i.   **James Blackburn McGrew** was born on 21 Mar 1781 in Adams County, Pennsylvania, died on 4 Oct 1836 in West Newton, Westmoreland, Pennsylvania at age 55, and was buried in Friends Burial Ground.

4 F   ii.   **Deborah McGrew** was born on 6 Sep 1783 in Adams County, Pennsylvania, died on 16 Aug 1855 in Fayette City, Fayette County, Pennsylvania at age 71, and was buried in Friends Burial Ground.

5 M   iii.   **Simon Blackburn McGrew** was born on 14 Feb 1788 in York County, Pennsylvania, died on 9 Oct 1854 in Westmoreland County, Pennsylvania at age 66, and was buried in Friends Burial Ground.

6 M   iv.   **Thomas Blackburn McGrew** was born on 11 Mar 1792 in York County, Pennsylvania, died on 10 Mar 1857 in Hamilton County, Ohio at age 64, and was buried in Wesleyan Cemetery.

7 M   v.   **Dr. John Blackburn McGrew** was born on 7 May 1795 in Westmoreland County, Pennsylvania, died in 1865 in Harrison County, Ohio at age 70, and was buried in Longview Cemetery.

+ 8 M   vi. **Archibald Blackburn McGrew** was born on 26 Dec 1799 in Sewickley, Westmoreland County, Pennsylvania and died on 11 Jan 1843 in Sewickley, Westmoreland County, Pennsylvania at age 43.

Third Generation (Grandchildren)

8. Archibald Blackburn McGrew *(James Blackburn Baird [2], James [1])* was born on 26 Dec 1799 in Sewickley, Westmoreland County, Pennsylvania and died on 11 Jan 1843 in Sewickley, Westmoreland County, Pennsylvania at age 43.

Archibald married **Susannah Gilbert,** daughter of **Abner Gilbert** and **Ann Cooper,** on 26 Dec 1822 in Sewickley, Westmoreland County, Pennsylvania. Susannah was born on 12 Mar 1804 in Sewickley, Westmoreland County, Pennsylvania and died on 14 Sep 1873 in Allegheny County, Pennsylvania at age 69.

Children from this marriage were:

9 F   i. **Philena Wakefield McGrew** was born on 14 Oct 1823 in Westmoreland County, Pennsylvania and died on 15 Dec 1889 in Wesley Township, Washington, Ohio at age 66.

Philena married **William Graham**.

Philena

Philena next married **Samuel Lytle**.

10 M   ii. **Abner Gilbert McGrew** was born on 27 Feb 1826 in Westmoreland County, Pennsylvania and died in Aug 1890 at age 64.

Abner married **Mary Ann Brunner** on 11 Jun 1846 in Westmoreland County, Pennsylvania. Mary was born in 1827 and died on 17 Oct 1850 at age 23.

Albert Gilbert McGrew

Abner next married **Sophia Frances McWilliams** on 27 Nov 1851 in Westmoreland County, Pennsylvania. Sophia was born on 17 Feb 1829 in Pennsylvania and died on 6 Jan 1912 in Pittsburgh, Allegheny, Pennsylvania at age 82.

11 F   iii. **Elizabeth McGrew** was born on 11 Nov 1827 in Westmoreland County, Pennsylvania and died on 24 Jun 1900 in West Newton, Westmoreland, Pennsylvania at age 72.

Elizabeth married **Abraham Blackburn**.

12   F   iv.   **Margaret Ann McGrew** was born on 19 Oct 1829 in Sewickley, Westmoreland, Pennsylvania and died on 10 Apr 1902 at age 72.

Margaret married **John Ingraham**.

13   F   v.   **Mary Jane McGrew** was born on 29 Jan 1832 in Sewickley, Westmoreland, Pennsylvania and died on 16 Sep 1908 in What Cheer, Keokuk, Iowa at age 76.

Mary married **Eli Price**.

+ 14   M   vi.   **Benjamin Gilbert McGrew** was born on 31 Mar 1834 in Westmoreland County, Pennsylvania, died on 3 Aug 1904 in Allegheny County, Pennsylvania at age 70, and was buried in Saint Clair Cemetery.

15   F   vii.   **Deborah McGrew** was born on 2 Jan 1836 in Westmoreland County, Pennsylvania and died in Jan 1902 in City, Guernsey, Ohio at age 66.

Deborah married **Franklin J. McKain** on 29 Dec 1865 in Westmoreland County, Pennsylvania. Franklin was born on 25 Sep 1842 and died on 3 Feb 1923 at age 80.

Deborah McGrew

16   F   viii.   **Isabella McGrew** was born on 29 Mar 1837 in Westmoreland County, Pennsylvania.

Isabella married **J. W. Blackburn**.

17   F   ix.   **Rebecca McGrew** was born on 28 Aug 1838 in Westmoreland County, Pennsylvania and died on 7 Feb 1925 in West Newton, Westmoreland, Pennsylvania at age 86.

Rebecca married **Jacob W. Greenawalt** in 1860. Jacob was born on 27 Oct 1837 and died on 17 May 1864 at age 26.

18   F   x.   **Phebe Catherine McGrew** was born on 7 Jul 1840 in Westmoreland County, Pennsylvania and died on 31 Mar 1932 in Washington County, Ohio at age 91.

Phebe married **James Emmor Shanor** in 1858. James was born on 25 Sep 1838.

19   M   xi.   **James McGrew** was born on 1 Mar 1842 in Westmoreland County, Pennsylvania and died on 31 Dec 1842 in Westmoreland County, Pennsylvania.

Fourth Generation (Great-Grandchildren)

14. Benjamin Gilbert McGrew *(Archibald Blackburn [3], James Blackburn Baird [2], James [1])* was born on 31 Mar 1834 in Westmoreland County, Pennsylvania, died on 3 Aug 1904 in Allegheny County, Pennsylvania at age 70, and was buried in Saint Clair Cemetery.

Benjamin married **Katherine Sowash "Kate" Howell,** daughter of **John Arnold Howell** and **Sarah Sowash,** on 17 Nov 1857 in Turtle Creek, Allegheny County, Pennsylvania. Katherine was born on 31 Mar 1839 in Allegheny County, Pennsylvania, died on 8 Jan 1910 in Pittsburgh, Allegheny County, Pennsylvania at age 70, and was buried in Saint Clair Cemetery.

Benjamin Gilbert McGrew

Children from this marriage were:

20 F i. **Minerva Etta McGrew** was born on 9 Sep 1858 and died on 9 Dec 1927 at age 69.

Minerva married **John Pollock Douglass** on 1 Feb 1881. John was born on 20 Apr 1856 and died on 1 Aug 1934 at age 78.

21 M ii. **John Franklin McGrew** was born in 1859, died on 20 May 1910 at age 51, and was buried in Saint Clair Cemetery.

+ 22 M iii. **Archibald Benjamin McGrew Sr.** was born on 29 Mar 1861 in Westmoreland County, Pennsylvania, died on 14 Apr 1919 in Greensburg, Westmoreland County, Pennsylvania at age 58, and was buried in Saint Clair Cemetery.

23 M iv. **Dilwyn Gilbert McGrew** was born on 14 Sep 1864, died on 15 Nov 1923 at age 59, and was buried in Saint Clair Cemetery.

24 M v. **William Edgar McGrew** was born in 1866 and died on 15 Jan 1913 at age 47.

William married **Carrie E. Kramer**. Carrie died on 15 May 1929.

25 F vi. **Sarah Shirwell McGrew** was born on 29 Dec 1867 and died on 25 Dec 1951 at age 83.

26 F vii. **Susan Belle McGrew** was born on 7 Mar 1870 and died on 14 Apr 1937 at age 67.

Susan married **Franklin Ball Adams** on 10 Jan 1895. Franklin died in Nov 1918.

27 M viii. **Wesley Cope McGrew** was born on 24 Mar 1875 and died on 15 Mar 1946 at age 70.

Wesley married **Elma Adelaide Marian Johnson** on 17 Apr 1900. Elma was born on 13 Jan 1873 and died on 24 Feb 1930 at age 57.

Fifth Generation (2nd Great-Grandchildren)

22. Archibald Benjamin McGrew Sr. *(Benjamin Gilbert [4], Archibald Blackburn [3], James Blackburn Baird [2], James [1])* was born on 29 Mar 1861 in Westmoreland County, Pennsylvania, died on 14 Apr 1919 in Greensburg, Westmoreland County, Pennsylvania at age 58, and was buried in Saint Clair Cemetery.

Archibald married **Minnie E. Leasure,** daughter of **Rev. Loren Bigelow Leasure** and **Anna Overholt Tintsman,** on 23 Oct 1883 in Greensburg, Westmoreland County, Pennsylvania. Minnie was born on 21 Jan 1864 in Westmoreland County, Pennsylvania, died on 28 Jun 1952 in Westmoreland County, Pennsylvania at age 88, and was buried in Saint Clair Cemetery.

Children from this marriage were:

28   F   i.   **Lillian E. McGrew** was born on 16 May 1885 in Greensburg, Westmoreland County, Pennsylvania, died in 1940 in Greensburg, Westmoreland County, Pennsylvania at age 55, and was buried in Saint Clair Cemetery.

      Lillian married **Paul C. Lappe**. Paul was born in 1884, died in 1918 at age 34, and was buried in Saint Clair Cemetery.

29   M   ii.   **Roy Leasure McGrew** was born on 11 Feb 1888 in Greensburg, Westmoreland County, Pennsylvania, died on 28 May 1960 in Pittsburgh, Allegheny County, Pennsylvania at age 72, and was buried in Homewood Cemetery.

30　F　iii.　**May Tintsman McGrew** was born on 15 Apr 1890 in Westmoreland County, Pennsylvania, died in 1986 at age 96, and was buried in Saint Clair Cemetery.

May married **Frank Sands**. Frank was born in 1882, died in 1960 at age 78, and was buried in Saint Clair Cemetery.

31　M　iv.　**Archibald Benjamin McGrew Jr** was born on 2 Feb 1893 in Greensburg, Westmoreland County, Pennsylvania, died on 6 Dec 1973 in Indiana, Indiana County, Pennsylvania at age 80, and was buried in Oakland Cemetery and Mausoleum.

Archibald married **Virginia Hall**.

32　F　v.　**Minnie Emma McGrew** was born on 20 Jul 1895 in Greensburg, Westmoreland County, Pennsylvania, died on 13 Oct 1982 in Pittsburgh, Allegheny County, Pennsylvania at age 87, and was buried in Homewood Cemetery.

+　33　M　vi.　**Albert Douthett McGrew** was born on 22 Jan 1898 in Greensburg, Westmoreland County, Pennsylvania, died on 13 Jul 1998 in Kerr County, Texas at age 100, and was buried in Fenlons Cemetery Mackinac County, Michigan.

34　F　vii.　**Helen Overholt McGrew** was born on 6 Oct 1901 in Westmoreland County, Pennsylvania, died in 1981 at age 80, and was buried in Saint Clair Cemetery.

Sixth Generation (3rd Great-Grandchildren)

33. Albert Douthett McGrew *(Archibald Benjamin Sr. [5], Benjamin Gilbert [4], Archibald Blackburn [3], James Blackburn Baird [2], James [1])* was born on 22 Jan 1898 in Greensburg, Westmoreland County, Pennsylvania, died on 13 Jul 1998 in Kerr County, Texas at age 100, and was buried in Fenlons Cemetery Mackinac County, Michigan.

Albert married **Bertha Marie Fenlon,** daughter of **Joseph Patrick Fenlon** and **Emily Hintz,** on 14 Feb 1924 in Wayne, Mackinac, Michigan. Bertha was born on 9 Jun 1898 in Hessel, Mackinac County, Michigan, died on 7 Apr 1993 in Alpine, Brewster, Texas at age 94, and was buried in Fenlons Cemetery Mackinac County, Michigan.

Children from this marriage were:

35 F i. **Anne Leasure McGrew** was born on 2 Jan 1926 in Pittsburgh, Allegheny County, Pennsylvania, died on 25 Dec 2011 in Walnut Creek, Contra Costa County, California at age 85, and was buried in Fenlons Cemetery.

+ 36 F ii. **Natalie Jane McGrew** was born on 20 Aug 1929 in Pittsburgh, Allegheny County, Pennsylvania.

37 F iii. **Mary Fenlon McGrew** was born on 18 Sep 1934 in Franklin, Venango County, Pennsylvania.

Mary married **Charles Gorham "Chuck" Brewer** on 14 Jan 1958 in Franklin, Venango County, Pennsylvania. Charles was born on 25 Apr 1927 in St Johns, Clinton, Michigan, died on 17 Dec 2008 in Smithfield, Johnston, North Carolina at age 81, and was buried in Cremated.

Seventh Generation (4th Great-Grandchildren)

36. Natalie Jane McGrew *(Albert Douthett [6], Archibald Benjamin Sr. [5], Benjamin Gilbert [4], Archibald Blackburn [3], James Blackburn Baird [2], James [1])* was born on 20 Aug 1929 in Pittsburgh, Allegheny County, Pennsylvania.

Natalie married **William C. Jaeck**, son of **Clifford Arthur Jaeck** and **Melania Cecelia McNerney**. William was born on 11 Jan 1930 in Toledo, Lucas County, Ohio.

Children from this marriage were:

  38 M   i. **William Albert Jaeck** was born on 24 Dec 1953 in Washington, DC.

+ 39 F   ii. **Shawna Marie Jaeck** was born on 9 Dec 1954 in Washington, DC.

  40 F   iii. **Kathleen Elizabeth Jaeck** was born on 12 Apr 1956 in Washington, DC.

Eighth Generation (5th Great-Grandchildren)

39. Shawna Marie Jaeck *(Natalie Jane McGrew [7], Albert Douthett [6], Archibald Benjamin Sr. [5], Benjamin Gilbert [4], Archibald Blackburn [3], James Blackburn Baird [2], James [1])* was born on 9 Dec 1954 in Washington, DC.

Shawna married **Warren Harold Hunt Jr** on 20 Aug 1977 in Canton, Stark County, Ohio. Warren was born on 30 Aug 1955 in Cleveland, Cuyahoga County, Ohio.

Children from this marriage were:

+ 41 F i. **Erika Marie Hunt** was born on 28 Mar 1982 in Pittsburgh, Allegheny County, Pennsylvania.

+ 42 M ii. **Jason Warren Hunt** was born on 6 Feb 1986 in Pittsburgh, Allegheny County, Pennsylvania.

Ninth Generation (6th Great-Grandchildren)

41. Erika Marie Hunt *(Shawna Marie Jaeck [8], Natalie Jane McGrew [7], Albert Douthett [6], Archibald Benjamin Sr. [5], Benjamin Gilbert [4], Archibald Blackburn [3], James Blackburn Baird [2], James [1])* was born on 28 Mar 1982 in Pittsburgh, Allegheny County, Pennsylvania.

Erika married **Jeremy Tyson Hasford** on 9 Oct 2009 in Mars, Butler County, Pennsylvania.

Children from this marriage were:

43 F i. **Evelyn Marie Hasford** was born on 22 Feb 2017.

44 F ii. **Clara Hope Hasford** was born on 15 Dec 2018.

42. Jason Warren Hunt *(Shawna Marie Jaeck [8], Natalie Jane McGrew [7], Albert Douthett [6], Archibald Benjamin Sr. [5], Benjamin Gilbert [4], Archibald Blackburn [3], James Blackburn Baird [2], James [1])* was born on 6 Feb 1986 in Pittsburgh, Allegheny County, Pennsylvania.

Jason married **Sara Holahan** on 31 Aug 2013 in Dayton, Montgomery County, Ohio.

The child from this marriage was:

45 F   i. **Cora Leigh Hunt** was born on 30 Sep 2018.

First Generation

46. John Fenlon was born in 1801, died in 1866 in County Carlow, Ireland at age 65, and was buried in St. Mary's Church of Ireland Church Cemetery unmarked.

> Research Notes: John Fenlon
> Ireland Civil Registration Indexes, 1845-1958
>
>
> Name:
> John Fenlon,Event Type: Death, Event Date:1866 Event Place:Carlow, Ireland
> Registration Quarter and Year:1866 Registration District: Carlow Age:65
> Birth Year (Estimated):   1801
> Volume Number:3
>
> John Fenlon
> Ireland, Petty Sessions Court Registers, 1828-1912
>
> Name:John Fenlon
> Event Type:Court
> Event Date 29 Oct 1860
> Event Place:Carlow, Ireland
> County: Carlow
> Role of Individual:Witness
> Court: Bagenalstown

John married **Ellen Scott**. Ellen was born in 1801, died in Apr 1881 in County Carlow, Ireland at age 80, and was buried in St. Mary's Church of Ireland Church Cemetery unmarked.

Children from this marriage were:

    47 M   i.   **James Fenlon** was born in County Carlow, Ireland.

                     James married **Mary Doyle** on 16 Oct 1865 in Bagenalstown, County Carlow, Ireland.

+ 48 M   ii. **Edward Fenlon** was born on 30 Apr 1826 in Bagenalstown, County Carlow, Ireland, was christened in May 1826, died on 8 Feb 1920 in Mackinac County, Michigan at age 93, and was buried in Fenlons Cemetery.

    49 F   iii. **Elizabeth Fenlon** was born about 1827 in County Carlow, Ireland.

                     Elizabeth married **Thomas Connors** on 22 Nov 1866 in Bagenalstown, County Carlow, Ireland.

Second Generation (Children)

48. Edward Fenlon *(John [1])* was born on 30 Apr 1826 in Bagenalstown, County Carlow, Ireland, was christened in May 1826, died on 8 Feb 1920 in Mackinac County, Michigan at age 93, and was buried in Fenlons Cemetery.

> Research Notes: Immigration Year   1886

Edward married **Mary Murphy,** daughter of **John Murphy** and **Ellen Tobey,** in 1855 in County Carlow, Ireland. Mary was born in Aug 1844 in Ireland, died on 17 Apr 1916 in Mackinac County, Michigan at age 71, and was buried in Fenlons Cemetery.

Children from this marriage were:

    50 M   i.   **John Fenlon** was born in 1856 in County Carlow, Ireland and died on 21 Jun 1941 in St Ignace, MacKinac County, Michigan at age 85.

                     John married **Anna Randall Merrill** on 8 Apr 1919 in Emmet, Michigan. Anna was born in 1863.

+ 51 M   ii. **Joseph Patrick Fenlon** was born on 17 Mar 1866 in Bagenalstown, County Carlow, Ireland, died on 18 Jan 1941 in Sault Sainte Marie, Chippewa County, Michigan at age 74, and was buried in Fenlons Cemetery.

+ 52 M   iii. **Edward Paul Fenlon** was born on 13 Jul 1870 in Bagenalstown, County Carlow, Ireland, died on 19 Jul 1943 in Mackinac County, Michigan at age 73, and was buried in Fenlons Cemetery.

    53 M   iv. **Thomas Fenlon** was born on 23 Aug 1870 in Kilcock, County Kildare, Ireland and died between Apr and Jun 1939

in County Carlow, Ireland.

54   F   v.   **Ellen Fenlon** was born in 1872 in County Carlow, Ireland and died in 1902 in Mackinac County, Michigan at age 30.

\+ 55   M   vi.   **William A. Fenlon** was born in May 1873 in Ireland, died on 23 Jun 1946 in Everett, Snohomish County, Washington at age 73, and was buried in Evergreen Cemetery.

56   F   vii.   **Bridget Fenlon** was born in 1874 in County Carlow, Ireland and died in 1883 at age 9.

\+ 57   M   viii.   **James Fenlon** was born on 20 Oct 1874 in Godgestown, Kildare, Ireland, died in 1910 in St Ignace, MacKinac County, Michigan at age 36, and was buried in Fenlons Cemetery.

\+ 58   M   ix.   **Michael Frances Fenlon** was born on 10 Oct 1880 in Godgestown, Kildare, Ireland and died after 1940 in Canada ??.

Third Generation (Grandchildren)

51. Joseph Patrick Fenlon *(Edward [2], John [1])* was born on 17 Mar 1866 in Bagenalstown, County Carlow, Ireland, died on 18 Jan 1941 in Sault Sainte Marie, Chippewa County, Michigan at age 74, and was buried in Fenlons Cemetery.

Research Notes: THE JOSEPH FENLON FAMILY Bertha Fenlon McGrew
Joseph Patrick Fenlon, a pioneer and resident of Mackinac County for 55 years, came from Ireland to Canada at the age of 16 together with his parents, seven brothers, and two sisters in 1882. They first settled in Seaforth, Ontario (north and slightly west of London), where they remained for 3 years. In 1885 Joseph and apparently brothers John and Edward migrated north to Sault Ste. Marie(probably via the Canadian Pacific steamer out of Owen Sound) and thence entered the US. It is said that at first they worked the lumber camps, probably the ones operated by Smith & Hossack near Rader and the Gogomain, whence Joseph walked, following lumber company tote roads and then the Indian trail that came out near the center of what now is Hessel, at the marina. The first sight that met his eyes was that of two Indian squaws in birch bark canoes lifting nets, which were filled with jumbo whitefish of a size no longer caught. The beauties and possibilities of the location so impressed him that, there and then he decided to settle near the spot. He must have returned to the Gogomain to lumber through the winter and then come back, with his brothers, in the spring. For in April of 1886 John and Edward filed side- by-side homesteads behind the Wendell owned shorefront and immediately north of those filed the previous year by Frank Pillman and David Stuart. Joseph filed for his in September north and slightly west of Mackinac Bay, behind the Wendells and George Andrews. Joseph first clerked for the Hessel family in their store, but in 1891 he and his younger brother James, it seems that by now the rest of the family had arrived, built a general store on the Hessel site of what is now the James Bowlby residence. Hessel Restaurant. This was a very traditional country store, though it later became principally a market, dealing in green groceries, produce, meat, and general merchandise, from basic hardware's, to fabrics to toys. This burned and rebuilt in 1908, operated as The Fenlon Brothers Stores until 1950, when it was first leased, then sold to Forrest B. Dick Church of Cedarville by Hintz Fenlon, Josephs son and heir to the store. Besides Hintz, Joseph had two daughter, Ellen (Mrs. Paul Tobin) later of Akron Ohio and Bertha (Mrs. Albert D. McGrew) of Franklin, Pennsylvania. (This is who Longs bought it from in October 1986) Unable to obtain land in Ireland as a Roman Catholic under English Protestant rule, Joseph was obsessed with the acquisition of property-as his means would permit. He thus often attended and invested at tax sales. As land was acquired with suitable timber on it, the Fenlon brothers engaged in the lumber business together with their retail trade enterprise, the one business complementing the other. James died at the age of 35 and was buried on the homestead where his parents could see his grave from the window of their home. Many of the Fenlon descendants are now buried there. The township eventually took over the burial ground, but it is still the Fenlon Cemetery. Joseph died in 1940 at age 74. Both Joseph and his son, Hintz, became fluent in the Chippewa language so that they could easily communicate with the local Indians, of whom there were a goodly number through the early days of this century. In 1907 or 08 Joseph, Hintz and Bertha were inducted into the local Chippwea band with appropriate ceremonies. A great feast was held at Chief Sabtigos home, the war dance was danced, and then the pipe of peace was smoked by all. The pipe was a beautiful article, its stem was covered with Indian symbols and the bowl was of red clay inclaid with pewter. Joseph was declared Chief of the White Men and given the name Ossowanimikee, which means Yellow Thunder. Hintz was Wasagesic and Bertha, Wasagesic go quay. Bertha now of McAllen Texas still used the old family home as a summer residence. The house was built in 1897 by Joseph Kramen, boat builder and part time carpenter, without benefit of either plumb bob or square.
Written by Albert D. McGrew

Descendants of John Fenlon

Joseph married **Emily Hintz,** daughter of **John C. Hintz** and **Emilie W. Kroplien,** on 25 Mar 1895 in St Ignace, MacKinac County, Michigan. Emily was born on 7 May 1871 in Mackinac County, Michigan, died on 5 Oct 1934 in Mackinac County, Michigan at age 63, and was buried in Fenlons Cemetery.

Children from this marriage were:

59 F   i.   **Ellen Louise Fenlon** was born on 31 Jan 1896 in Mackinac County, Michigan.

Ellen married **Paul W. Tobin** on 20 Aug 1921 in Mackinac County, Michigan. Paul was born in 1896 in Akron, Ohio.

60 M   ii.   **Hintz Joseph Fenlon** was born on 15 Feb 1897 in Mackinac County, Michigan, died on 21 Sep 1950 in Mackinac County, Michigan at age 53, and was buried in Fenlons Cemetery.

Hintz married **Edna McGregor** on 28 Jun 1922 in Mackinac County, Michigan.

Hintz Joseph Fenlon

+ 61 F   iii.   **Bertha Marie Fenlon** was born on 9 Jun 1898 in Hessel, Mackinac County, Michigan, died on 7 Apr 1993 in Alpine, Brewster, Texas at age 94, and was buried in Fenlons Cemetery Mackinac County, Michigan.

52. Edward Paul Fenlon *(Edward [2], John [1])* was born on 13 Jul 1870 in Bagenalstown, County Carlow, Ireland, died on 19 Jul 1943 in Mackinac County, Michigan at age 73, and was buried in Fenlons Cemetery.

Edward married **Effie Obeshaw**. Effie was born in 1876 in Michigan, died in 1945 in Mackinac County, Michigan at age 69, and was buried in Fenlons Cemetery.

Children from this marriage were:

62 M   i.   **Bernard J. Fenlon** was born on 13 Aug 1898 in Mackinac County, Michigan, died on 23 Jul 1971 in Mackinac County, Michigan at age 72, and was buried in Fenlons Cemetery.

63 M   ii.   **Terrance M. Fenlon** was born on 6 May 1901 in Mackinac County, Michigan, died on 7 Sep 1979 in Mackinac County, Michigan at age 78, and was buried in Fenlons Cemetery.

64 M   iii.   **Ernest E. Fenlon** was born in 1904 in Mackinac County, Michigan.

65 M   iv.   **Emmet E. Fenlon** was born on 20 Feb 1904 in Mackinac County, Michigan and died on 13 Apr 1991 in Pasco, Florida at age 87.

Emmet married **Frances Belford** on 3 Mar 1934 in Detroit, Wayne, Michigan. Frances was born circa 1911 in Kentucky.

66 M v. **Baby Boy Fenlon** was born on 2 Nov 1907 in Hessel, Mackinac County, Michigan, died on 3 Nov 1907 in Hessel, Mackinac County, Michigan, and was buried in Fenlons Cemetery.

67 F vi. **Margaret M. Fenlon** was born about 1909 in Mackinac County, Michigan.

Margaret married **Maurice Carr** on 6 Nov 1926 in St Ignace, MacKinac County, Michigan. Maurice was born about 1905 in Naubinway, New York.

68 F vii. **Stella A. Fenlon** was born about 1912 in Mackinac County, Michigan.

69 F viii. **Florence Elizabeth Fenlon** was born on 15 Oct 1912 in Hessel, Mackinac County, Michigan and died in 1960 in Detroit, Wayne, Michigan at age 48.

70 F ix. **Eileen L. Fenlon** was born on 4 Jun 1915 in Mackinac County, Michigan and died in Mar 1984 in Norfolk, Norfolk City County, Virginia at age 68.

71 M x. **Eleanor R. Fenlon** was born on 4 Jul 1917 in Hessel, Mackinac County, Michigan, died in Jan 1982 in Mackinac County, Michigan at age 64, and was buried in Fenlons Cemetery.

55. William A. Fenlon *(Edward[2], John[1])* was born in May 1873 in Ireland, died on 23 Jun 1946 in Everett, Snohomish County, Washington at age 73, and was buried in Evergreen Cemetery.

William married **Norah Gorman** on 13 Apr 1898 in St Ignace, MacKinac County, Michigan. Norah was born in Oct 1880 in Michigan, died on 26 Jun 1942 in Everett, Snohomish County, Washington at age 61, and was buried in Evergreen Cemetery.

The child from this marriage was:

72 M i. **James W. Fenlon** was born on 1 Dec 1914 in Everett, Snohomish County, Washington, died in May 1977 in Everett, Snohomish County, Washington at age 62, and was buried in Evergreen Cemetery.

57. James Fenlon *(Edward[2], John[1])* was born on 20 Oct 1874 in Godgestown, Kildare, Ireland, died in 1910 in St Ignace, MacKinac County, Michigan at age 36, and was buried in Fenlons Cemetery.

James married **Anna D. McLaughlin** on 7 Jan 1903 in St Ignace, MacKinac County, Michigan. Anna was born in Aug 1877 in Mackinac Island, Mackinac County, Michigan and died in Clark, Mackinac County, Michigan.

Children from this marriage were:

73 M   i.   **Edward Hugh Fenlon** was born on 7 Oct 1903 in St. Ignace, Mackinac County, Michigan and died on 19 Sep 2010 in Long Beach, Los Angeles County, California at age 106.

         Edward married **Elizabeth J. Weckbaugh** on 20 Feb 1939 in Saginaw, Saginaw County, Michigan. Elizabeth was born on 10 Jan 1914 in Saginaw, Saginaw County, Michigan and died on 10 Mar 2001 in Petoskey, Emmet County, Michigan at age 87.

74 F   ii.   **Catherine Mary (Kay) Fenlon** was born on 8 Jan 1905 in Mackinac County, Michigan and died on 26 Jul 1988 in Sault Sainte Marie, Chippewa County, Michigan at age 83.

75 F   iii.   **Genevieve Fenlon** was born in Jun 1905 in Mackinac County, Michigan.

76 M   iv.   **James Joseph Fenlon** was born on 10 Dec 1908 in Sault Ste. Marie, Chippewa County, Michigan and died on 13 Mar 1996 in Sault Sainte Marie, Chippewa County, Michigan at age 87.

58. Michael Frances Fenlon *(Edward [2], John [1])* was born on 10 Oct 1880 in Godgestown, Kildare, Ireland and died after 1940 in Canada ??.

     Research Notes: Divorces and is last found in Canada

Michael married **Anna B. Rhoads** on 31 Oct 1905 in St. Ignace, Mackinac County, Michigan. Anna was born in 1883 in Michigan, died in 1958 in Mackinac County, Michigan at age 75, and was buried in Saint Ignace.

Children from this marriage were:

77 M   i.   **Chambers M. Fenlon**.

78 F   ii.   **Nancy Anna C. Fenlon**.

79 F   iii.   **Elizabeth Fenlon** was born on 28 Feb 1909 in Saint Ignace, Mackinac, Michigan and died in Aug 1976 in Saint Ignace, Mackinac, Michigan at age 67.

80 F   iv.   **Frances Fenlon** was born about 1911 in Hessel, Mackinac County, Michigan.

         Frances married **Eugene L. Bolan** on 18 Jun 1932 in St Ignace, MacKinac County, Michigan.

81   M   v.   **John R. Fenlon** was born on 16 May 1913 in Mackinac County, Michigan, died in Dec 1994 in Mackinac County, Michigan at age 81, and was buried in Gros Cap Cemetery.

82   F   vi.   **Anna Catherine Fenlon** was born in 1915 in St Ignace, MacKinac County, Michigan, died in 1994 in St Ignace, MacKinac County, Michigan at age 79, and was buried in Saint Ignace.

83   F   vii.   **Mary Dorothy Fenlon** was born in 1918 in Mackinac County, Michigan, died in 2012 in Mackinac County, Michigan at age 94, and was buried in St Ignace.

84   F   viii.   **Helen Patricia Fenlon** was born on 18 Apr 1921 in Mackinac County, Michigan, died on 17 May 2006 in Mackinac County, Michigan at age 85, and was buried in St Ignace.

85   F   ix.   **Theresa Mary Fenlon** was born on 21 Oct 1927 in Mackinac County, Michigan, died on 7 Jun 2016 in East Jordan, Charlevoix County, Michigan at age 88, and was buried in St Ignace.

Fourth Generation (Great-Grandchildren)

61. Bertha Marie Fenlon *(Joseph Patrick [3], Edward [2], John [1])* was born on 9 Jun 1898 in Hessel, Mackinac County, Michigan, died on 7 Apr 1993 in Alpine, Brewster, Texas at age 94, and was buried in Fenlons Cemetery Mackinac County, Michigan.

Bertha married **Albert Douthett McGrew,** son of **Archibald Benjamin McGrew Sr.** and **Minnie E. Leasure,** on 14 Feb 1924 in Wayne, Mackinac, Michigan. Albert was born on 22 Jan 1898 in Greensburg, Westmoreland County, Pennsylvania, died on 13 Jul 1998 in Kerr County, Texas at age 100, and was buried in Fenlons Cemetery Mackinac County, Michigan.

(Duplicate Line. See Person 33 on Page 49)

Descendants of John Murphy

First Generation

86. John Murphy was born in 1791 in Ireland and died in 1871 in County Carlow, Ireland at age 80.

> Research Notes: Ireland Civil Registration Indexes, 1845-1958
> Name: John Murphy Event Type: Death Event Date: 1871 Event Place: Carlow, Ireland
> Registration Quarter and Year:1871 Registration District:Carlow
> Age:80 Birth Year (Estimated):1791
> Volume Number:3

John married **Ellen Tobey**. Ellen was born in 1829 in Ireland and died in Jan-Mar 1900 in County Carlow, Ireland at age 71.

The child from this marriage was:
+ 87 F   i.   **Mary Murphy** was born in Aug 1844 in Ireland, died on 17 Apr 1916 in Mackinac County, Michigan at age 71, and was buried in Fenlons Cemetery.

Second Generation (Children)

87. Mary Murphy *(John [1])* was born in Aug 1844 in Ireland, died on 17 Apr 1916 in Mackinac County, Michigan at age 71, and was buried in Fenlons Cemetery.

> Research Notes: Michigan Deaths and Burials, 1800-1995
> Name:Mary Fenlon Gender:FemaleDeath Date:17 Apr 1916
> Death Place:Clark Twp., Mackinac, Michigan Age:72 Birth Date:1844 Birthplace: Ireland
> Occupation:Housewife Race:White Marital Status:Married Father's Name:John Murphy Mother's Name: Ellen Tobey

Mary married **Edward Fenlon,** son of **John Fenlon** and **Ellen Scott,** in 1855 in County Carlow, Ireland. Edward was born on 30 Apr 1826 in Bagenalstown, County Carlow, Ireland, was christened in May 1826, died on 8 Feb 1920 in Mackinac County, Michigan at age 93, and was buried in Fenlons Cemetery.

(Duplicate Line. See Person 48 on Page 54)

First Generation

88. Abraham Leasure was born on 11 Apr 1695 in Switzerland, was christened on 13 Apr 1695, and died in 1785 in Westmoreland County, Pennsylvania at age 90.

Research Notes: About Abraham Leasure, I Rev. War Vet.
THE FOLLOWING INFORMATION WAS FURNISHED BY PHIL LASHER: Abraham's dates are b. 1695 d. 1785 in Bedford County. Some accounts have him living as late as 1790 but all have him as died in Bedford County. Also most Rev soldiers filed for a pension between 1785 and 1790 but Abraham did not.

The government veterans grave locator lists only two Leasure's in Unity cemetery (both Abraham b. 1713 d. 1803 & brother Georgeb. 1728 d. 1809 attached.) Abraham b. 1713 d. 1803 and his wife Margaret b. 1715 d. 1818 both died and were buried on their farm Westmoreland County, near the present site of the Westmoreland county fair grounds. Their bodies were moved at a later date to the unity cemetery, and buried next to his brother George.

The government veterans grave locator lists only two Leasure's in Unity cemetery (both Abraham b. 1713 d. 1803 & brother Georgeb. 1728 d. 1809 attached.) Abraham b. 1713 d. 1803 and his wife Margaret b. 1715 d. 1818 both died and were buried on their farm Westmoreland County, near the present site of the Westmoreland county fair grounds. Their bodies were moved at a later date to the unity cemetery, and buried next to his brother George.

I am still looking for Abrahams records at the national archives and if they are ever found I will let you know where he is buried but we can be sure it is not in Unity cemetery.

Note: Abraham came from Novarri, France in 1754. He was a French Huguenot. Abraham was married to Margarette. The original spelling of his name was LeSouer or LeSueur

We can show that all his sons served in the same unit from Upper Dauphin Co., Pa., as did he in the Revolution. All his sons received their Revolutionary War bounty property in Westmoreland County except for Benjamin who became Lasher. The Westmoreland property can be traced to the bounty property given to the vary unit from Upper Dauphin Co., Pa., that they all served in.

Rev. A. Stapleton one of the first pastors in Westmoreland county wrote:

BIOGRAPHY: Rev. A. Stapleton, in his memorial of the Huguenots in America, gives the following concerning the Leasure family: "The Leasure family is both ancient and honorable, and was originally seated in the Province of Navarre, France. At the Revocation a branch of this family was compelled to flee to Switzerland for safety, and from whence came Abraham Leasure, who arrived in America in 1754, and located in upper Dauphin County, Pa., where the family name is still extant. A son of the immigrant located in Westmoreland County, Pa., where his descendants became prominent, notably Gen. Daniel Leasure, a distinguished officer of the Civil War ." (Stewart's History)

Thanks Phil Lasher

Father: Pierre LESUEUR b: ABT 1669 in Switzerland Mother: Jeanne DROUOT b: ABT 1671 in Basel, Switzerland

Marriage 1 MARGARETTE b: ABT 1691 in France Married: 1713 Children Has No Children Abraham LEASURE b: BET 1712 AND 1713 in Basel, Switzerland Has No Children Peter LEASURE b: ABT 1719 in Basel, Switzerland Has No Children Margaret LEASURE b: ABT 1725 in Basel, Switzerland Has Children George LEASURE b: 3 NOV 1728 in Basel, Switzerland Has No Children John LEASURE b: 1731 in Basel, Switzerland

There is much confusion and controversy both in regard to the place of Abrahams birth (Ancestry; Neatherlands, others France and findagrave; Switzerland) and, secondly, his father (Ancestry; Abraham, Our Family; Pierre, My Heritage; Jean Francois)

Abraham married **Margarette Poinsett**. Margarette was born in 1691 in France and died in Westmoreland County, Pennsylvania.

The child from this marriage was:
+ 89   M   i.   **Abraham Leasure** was born in Feb 1713 in Basel, Basel-Stadt, Basel-Stadt, Switzerland, died on 15 Mar 1803 in Leasureville, Butler County, Pennsylvania at age 90, and was buried in Unity Cemetery.

Second Generation (Children)

89. Abraham Leasure *(Abraham [1])* was born in Feb 1713 in Basel, Basel-Stadt, Basel-Stadt, Switzerland, died on 15 Mar 1803 in Leasureville, Butler County, Pennsylvania at age 90, and was buried in Unity Cemetery.

Research Notes: easure, — The Leasure family is both ancient and honorable, and was originally seated in the province of Navarre. At the Revocation a branch of this family was compelled to flee to Switzerland for safety, and from whence came Abraham Leasure, who arrived in 1754, and located in upper Dauphin county, where the family name is still extant. A son of the immigrant located in Westmoreland county where his descendants became prominent, notably General Daniel Leasure, a distinguished officer of the Civil war.

Abraham married **Margaret Marshall**. Margaret was born in 1715 in France, died on 15 Mar 1818 in Westmoreland County, Pennsylvania at age 103, and was buried in Unity Cemetery.

The child from this marriage was:
+ 90   M   i.   **Daniel Leasure** was born in 1758 in York County, Pennsylvania, died on 9 Dec 1830 in Mount Pleasant, Westmoreland County, Pennsylvania at age 72, and was buried in Middle Presbyterian Cemetery.

Third Generation (Grandchildren)

90. Daniel Leasure *(Abraham [2], Abraham [1])* was born in 1758 in York County, Pennsylvania, died on 9 Dec 1830 in Mount Pleasant, Westmoreland County, Pennsylvania at age 72, and was buried in Middle Presbyterian Cemetery.

Research Notes: Died-On the 8th inst, at his residence in Mount Pleasant township, Mr. DANIEL LEASURE, at an advanced age.

From: The Greensburg Gazette, Greensburg, Pennsylvania, on Friday December 17, 1830, Page 3

Note: Paper says he died the 8th and the headstone says the 9th.

Married: Elizabeth Ryan, about 1783

Daniel married **Elizabeth Reynolds,** daughter of **Joshua Reynolds** and **Rachel Kilgore,** in 1783. Elizabeth was born in 1768, died on 5 Sep 1840 in Mount Pleasant, Westmoreland County, Pennsylvania at age 72, and was buried in Middle Presbyterian Cemetery.

The child from this marriage was:
+ 91   M   i.   **Abraham Leasure** was born on 19 Jun 1786 in Greensburg, Westmoreland County, Pennsylvania, died on 29 Apr 1839 in Hempfield Township, Westmoreland County, Pennsylvania at age 52, and was buried in Sewickley Union Cemetery Association.

Fourth Generation (Great-Grandchildren)

91. Abraham Leasure *(Daniel [3], Abraham [2], Abraham [1])* was born on 19 Jun 1786 in Greensburg, Westmoreland County, Pennsylvania, died on 29 Apr 1839 in Hempfield Township, Westmoreland County, Pennsylvania at age 52, and was buried in Sewickley Union Cemetery Association.

Abraham married **Barbara Anna Lobingier**, daughter of **Christopher Lobingier Jr.** and **Elizabeth Mueller**. Barbara was born on 22 Feb 1786 in Laurelville, Westmoreland County, Pennsylvania, died on 6 Apr 1863 in Hempfield Township, Westmoreland County, Pennsylvania at age 77, and was buried in Sewickley Union Cemetery Association.

The child from this marriage was:
+ 92   M   i.   **Rev. Loren Bigelow Leasure** was born on 26 Oct 1826 in Madison, Westmoreland County, Pennsylvania, died on 9 Nov 1881 in Greensburg, Westmoreland County, Pennsylvania at age 55, and was buried in Saint Clair Cemetery.

Fifth Generation (2nd Great-Grandchildren)

92. Rev. Loren Bigelow Leasure *(Abraham [4], Daniel [3], Abraham [2], Abraham [1])* was born on 26 Oct 1826 in Madison, Westmoreland County, Pennsylvania, died on 9 Nov 1881 in Greensburg, Westmoreland County, Pennsylvania at age 55, and was buried in Saint Clair Cemetery.

Loren married **Anna Overholt Tintsman,** daughter of **John Tintsman** and **Anna Stauffer Overholt,** on 26 Nov 1855. Anna was born on 29 Dec 1838 in Westmoreland County, Pennsylvania, died on 31 Jul 1941 in Greensburg, Westmoreland County, Pennsylvania at age 102, and was buried in Saint Clair Cemetery.

Anna Overholt Tintsman

Children from this marriage were:

93   F   i. **Mariah Elizabeth Leasure** was born on 20 Oct 1857 in Irwin, Westmoreland County, Pennsylvania, died on 8 Aug 1938 in Jeannette, Westmoreland County, Pennsylvania at age 80, and was buried in Brush Creek Cemetery.

94   M   ii. **Israel Painter Leasure** was born on 11 Oct 1859 in Hempfield Township, Westmoreland County, Pennsylvania,, died on 21 Jan 1939 in Greensburg, Westmoreland County, Pennsylvania at age 79, and was buried in Union Cemetery.

Israel married **Emma Jane Stark** on 20 Feb 1883 in Pennsylvania. Emma was born on 22 Apr 1861 in Greensburg, Westmoreland County, Pennsylvania, died in Greensburg, Westmoreland County, Pennsylvania, and was buried in Union Cemetery.

95 F iii. **Ida Leasure** was born on 24 Nov 1861 in Greensburg, Westmoreland County, Pennsylvania, died on 7 Feb 1946 in Greensburg, Westmoreland County, Pennsylvania at age 84, and was buried in Saint Clair Cemetery.

+ 96 F iv. **Minnie E. Leasure** was born on 21 Jan 1864 in Westmoreland County, Pennsylvania, died on 28 Jun 1952 in Westmoreland County, Pennsylvania at age 88, and was buried in Saint Clair Cemetery.

97 F v. **Anna O. Leasure** was born in 1866 in Greensburg, Westmoreland County, Pennsylvania, died in 1885 in Greensburg, Westmoreland County, Pennsylvania at age 19, and was buried in Saint Clair Cemetery.

98 M vi. **Loran Bigelow Leasure Jr** was born in 1870 in Greensburg, Westmoreland County, Pennsylvania, died in 1957 in Greensburg, Westmoreland County, Pennsylvania at age 87, and was buried in Saint Clair Cemetery.

99 F vii. **Edna Leasure** was born in 1874 in Greensburg, Westmoreland County, Pennsylvania, died in 1971 in Greensburg, Westmoreland County, Pennsylvania at age 97, and was buried in Saint Clair Cemetery.

Descendants of Abraham Leasure

100 M viii. **John F. Leasure** was born on 13 Jun 1877 in Greensburg, Westmoreland County, Pennsylvania, died in Aug 1965 in Greensburg, Westmoreland County, Pennsylvania at age 88, and was buried in Saint Clair Cemetery.

Sixth Generation (3rd Great-Grandchildren)

96. Minnie E. Leasure *(Loren Bigelow (Rev.) [5], Abraham [4], Daniel [3], Abraham [2], Abraham [1])* was born on 21 Jan 1864 in Westmoreland County, Pennsylvania, died on 28 Jun 1952 in Westmoreland County, Pennsylvania at age 88, and was buried in Saint Clair Cemetery.

Minnie married **Archibald Benjamin McGrew Sr.,** son of **Benjamin Gilbert McGrew** and **Katherine Sowash "Kate" Howell,** on 23 Oct 1883 in Greensburg, Westmoreland County, Pennsylvania. Archibald was born on 29 Mar 1861 in Westmoreland County, Pennsylvania, died on 14 Apr 1919 in Greensburg, Westmoreland County, Pennsylvania at age 58, and was buried in Saint Clair Cemetery.

(Duplicate Line. See Person 22 on Page 48)

First Generation

101. Captain John George Mueller was born in 1715 in Sw Zurich, Switzerland and died in 1765 in Lebanon township, Pennsylvania at age 50.

> Research Notes: Title: Commemorative biographical encyclopedia of Dauphin County, Pennsylvania: containing sketches of prominent and representative citizens, and many of the early Scotch-Irish and German settlers.
> Authors: Anonymous
> City of Publication: Chambersburg, Pa.
> Publisher: J.M. Runk
> Date: 1896
> Page Count: 1223
> Notes: "In the compilation of the biographies we were ably assisted by William H. Egle ... A.S. Dudley ... Harry I. Huber ... R.H. Schively."
> Includes index.
> ports. ;
> Reel/Fiche Number: Genealogy & local history; LH 975
> Subject Headings: Dauphin County (Pa.) -- Biography.
> Pennsylvania -- Dauphin County
>
> Biographical Encyclopedia of Dauphin County - found on page 171
>
> Muller, John George, son of Rudolph Muller (more frequently writer Miller), was born September 21, 1715, in the Canton of Zurich, Switzerland; emigrated with his family to America in 1752, and settled in Lebanon township, Lancaster county, Province of Pennsylvania. He took the oath of allegiance October 23, 1752. He had been an officer in the Swiss service, and when the French and Indian war broke out he was commissioned a lieutenant in Col. James Burd's regiment of Provincial forces, May 8, 1760 (see Penn'a Arch. 2d ser., vol. ii, p605), promoted to a captaincy on the northern frontiers. October 12, 1764 (ib. p. 615). Captain Muller died April 19, 1765, in Lebanon township, leaving a wife Barbara Gloninger, who survived her husband several years, dying in 1783.

John married **Barbara Gloninger**.

The child from this marriage was:

+ 102 F   i. **Elizabeth Mueller** was born on 13 Jun 1744, died on 6 Sep 1815 in Stoystown, Somerset County, Pennsylvania at age 71, and was buried in IOOF Cemetery.

Second Generation (Children)

102. Elizabeth Mueller *(John George (Captain)* [1]*)* was born on 13 Jun 1744, died on 6 Sep 1815 in Stoystown, Somerset County, Pennsylvania at age 71, and was buried in IOOF Cemetery.

Elizabeth married **Christopher Lobingier Jr.**, son of **Christopher Lobingier** and **Anna Catherine Hubele**. Christopher was born on 4 Oct 1741 in Lancaster County, Pennsylvania, died on 4 Jul 1798 in Mount Pleasant, Westmoreland County, Pennsylvania at age 56, and was buried in Ridge Churches Union Cemetery.

The child from this marriage was:

+ 103 F   i. **Barbara Anna Lobingier** was born on 22 Feb 1786 in Laurelville, Westmoreland County, Pennsylvania, died on 6 Apr 1863 in Hempfield Township, Westmoreland County, Pennsylvania at age 77, and was buried in Sewickley Union Cemetery Association.

Third Generation (Grandchildren)

103. Barbara Anna Lobingier *(Elizabeth Mueller* [2]*, John George (Captain)* [1]*)* was born on 22 Feb 1786 in Laurelville, Westmoreland County, Pennsylvania, died on 6 Apr 1863 in Hempfield Township, Westmoreland County, Pennsylvania at age 77, and was buried in Sewickley Union Cemetery Association.

Barbara married **Abraham Leasure**, son of **Daniel Leasure** and **Elizabeth Reynolds**. Abraham was born on 19 Jun 1786 in Greensburg, Westmoreland County, Pennsylvania, died on 29 Apr 1839 in Hempfield Township, Westmoreland County, Pennsylvania at age 52, and was buried in Sewickley Union Cemetery Association.

(Duplicate Line. See Person 91 on Page 62)

First Generation

104. Christopher Lobingier was born circa 1700 in Wittenberg, Germany and died circa 1772 in Hummelstown, Dauphin County, Pennsylvania about age 72.

Research Notes: Source: Vince Gerheim . According to this source, Christopher LOBINGER immigrated to Philadelphia on September 18, 1727 on the ship William and Sara[h]. If this source is correct, then Christopher's surname, as reported on the ship's passenger list, was either LABENGYGER or LAMBENGYGER. See the ship's passenger lists cited below.

(2) Immigrants in Pennsylvania from 1727 to 1776 [database online], Provo, UT: Ancestry.com, 2001:

At a meeting of the Board of the Provincial Council, held at the Court House in Philadelphia, Sept. 21, 1727, one hundred and nine Palatines appeared, who, with their families, numbered about four hundred persons. These were imported into the Province in the ship William and Sarah, William Hill, Master, from Rotterdam, last from Dover, England, as by clearance from the officers of His Majesty's customs there. The said Master being asked if he had any license from the Court of Great Britain for transporting those people, and what their intentions were in coming hither, said that he had no license or allowance for their transportation other than the above clearance, and that he believed they designed to settle in this Province.--Col. Rec. III. 283.

ID Number: MH:N750

MH:I2875

N726All male persons above the age of sixteen did repeat and subscribe their names, or made their mark, to the following Declaration: "We subscribers, natives and late inhabitants of the Palatinate upon the Rhine and places adjacent, having transported ourselves and families into this Province of Pennsylvania, a colony subject to the crown of Great Britain, in hopes and expectation of finding a retreat and peaceable settlement therein, Do solemnly promise and engage, that we will be faithful and bear true allegiance to His present Majesty, King George THE SECOND, and His successors, kings of GreatBritain, and will be faithful to the proprietor of this Province; and that we will demean ourselves peaceably to all His said Majesty 's subjects, and strictly observe and conform to the Laws of England and of this Province, to the utmost of our power and the best of our understanding." . . .

In vol. iii. 284. Colonial Records, it is stated, "sundry of these foreigners lying sick on board, never came to be qualified." I have compared Lists A, B and C and find in List A, besides those givenabove, the following names: . . .

Christopher Labengyger, name written by clerk

ID Number: MH:N751

MH:I2875

N727(3) The Olive Tree Genealogy :

Palatine Ship WILLIAM AND SARAH 1727

William Hill, Master from Rotterdam, to Philadelphia 18th Sept. 1727

Name: Christopher Lambengyger

persons in party: 2

ID Number: MH:N752

MH:I2875

N728(4) Boucher, John Newton, A Century and a Half of Pittsburg[h] and Her People, New York, NY: Lewis Publishing Company, 1908, vol. 3, p. 229:

Christopher Lobingier, Sr. . . . was the founder of the family in this country. He with his brother Jacob emigrated from Wittenberg, Germany, prior to 1735, settling at Hummelstown, which was then in the territory embraced within Lancaster county, Pennsylvania, but which is now located in Dauphin county. The tradition in the family is that he was of French extraction, his forebears having been driven from France during the Huguenot persecution. They sought a refuge in Germany, and it was from that country that Christopher Lobingier and his brother started to found new homes in America. Soon after his arrival in this country Jacob disappeared while fighting the Indians and all trace of him was lost, the supposition being that he was killed by the savages. Christopher became an influential citizen and died where he located on his arrival in this country: He was buried in the old churchyard at Hummelstown, where his grave is still to be found, together with other members of his family.

ID Number: MH:N753

MH:I2875

N729(4) Boucher, John N., History of Westmoreland County, Pennsylvania, New York, NY: Lewis Publishing Co., 1906: Vol. 2, p. 64: Christopher Lobingier . . . came from Mecklenberg, Germany, and settled in [Lancaster now] Dauphin county. He was married before leaving Germany. Little is known of him except that he was a farmer, and that both he and his wife died, and are buried in Dauphin county. They had one son, Christopher. . . .Vol. 2, p. 485: Christopher Lobingier . . . came from Mecklenburg, Germany, and settled in [Lancaster now] Dauphin county, Pennsylvania. Vol. 3, p. 298: Christopher Lobingier, Sr. . . . was the founder of this family in the United States. He was a native of Wittenberg, Germany, and emigrated with his brother Jacob from the Fatherland prior to 1735, settling in Harrisburg, Lancaster county, Pennsylvania.

[Note by compiler: This source is ambiguous as to the birthplace of Christopher LOBINGIER. In several places, this source states that Christopher "came from Mecklenburg;" this could mean that (1) Christopher was born there or (2) Christopher was there before he came to America. In another place, this source states that Christopher "was a native of Wittenberg." Mecklenburg is a populated place in Mecklenburg-Vorpommern, Germany; and Wittenberg is a populated place in Baden-Württemberg, Germany.]

Christopher married **Anna Catherine Hubele**.

The child from this marriage was:

+ 105　M　　i. **Christopher Lobingier Jr.** was born on 4 Oct 1741 in Lancaster County, Pennsylvania, died on 4 Jul 1798 in Mount Pleasant, Westmoreland County, Pennsylvania at age 56, and was buried in Ridge Churches Union Cemetery.

Second Generation (Children)

105. Christopher Lobingier Jr. *(Christopher [1])* was born on 4 Oct 1741 in Lancaster County, Pennsylvania, died on 4 Jul 1798 in Mount Pleasant, Westmoreland County, Pennsylvania at age 56, and was buried in Ridge Churches Union Cemetery.

Christopher married **Elizabeth Mueller**, daughter of **Captain John George Mueller** and **Barbara Gloninger**. Elizabeth was born on 13 Jun 1744, died on 6 Sep 1815 in Stoystown, Somerset County, Pennsylvania at age 71, and was buried in IOOF Cemetery.

(Duplicate Line. See Person 102 on Page 66)

Descendants of Matthias Tintsman/Dinstman

First Generation

106. Matthias Tintsman/Dinstman was born about 1726 in Germany.

Matthias married **Aylse**.

The child from this marriage was:
+ 107 M   i.   **Adam Tintsman/Dinstman** was born in 1746 in Germany and died before 1813 in Westmoreland County, Pennsylvania.

Second Generation (Children)

107. Adam Tintsman/Dinstman *(Matthias [1])* was born in 1746 in Germany and died before 1813 in Westmoreland County, Pennsylvania.

Adam married **Elizabeth Anna Wismer**. Elizabeth was born circa 1750 and died on 18 Oct 1824 in Westmoreland County, Pennsylvania about age 74.

The child from this marriage was:
+ 108 M   i.   **John Tintsman/Dinstman** was born on 21 Aug 1778 in Bucks County, Pennsylvania and died on 8 May 1849 in Harmony, Susquehanna, Pennsylvania at age 70.

Third Generation (Grandchildren)

108. John Tintsman/Dinstman *(Adam [2], Matthias [1])* was born on 21 Aug 1778 in Bucks County, Pennsylvania and died on 8 May 1849 in Harmony, Susquehanna, Pennsylvania at age 70.

John married **Frances Stauffer**, daughter of **Abraham Stauffer** and **Anna Nissley**. Frances was born on 6 Apr 1783 in Bucks County, Pennsylvania and died on 27 May 1869 in Beaver, Mahoning, Ohio at age 86.

Children from this marriage were:
   109 F   i.   **Anna F. Tintsman** was born in 1806 in Westmoreland County, Pennsylvania and died in 1881 in Adams County, Illinois at age 75.

+ 110 M   ii.   **John Tintsman** was born on 1 Jul 1812 in Westmoreland County, Pennsylvania, died on 29 Mar 1866 in Westmoreland County, Pennsylvania at age 53, and was buried in Mount Pleasant, Westmoreland County, Pennsylvania.

Fourth Generation (Great-Grandchildren)

110. John Tintsman *(John [3], Adam [2], Matthias [1])* was born on 1 Jul 1812 in Westmoreland County, Pennsylvania, died on 29 Mar 1866 in Westmoreland County, Pennsylvania at age 53, and was buried in Mount Pleasant, Westmoreland County, Pennsylvania.

John married **Anna Stauffer Overholt**, daughter of **Abraham Overholt** and **Maria Stauffer**. Anna was born on 4 Jul 1812 in Westoverton, Pennsylvania and died on 29 Mar 1866 in Fayette City, Fayette County, Pennsylvania at age 53.

The child from this marriage was:
+ 111 F   i.   **Anna Overholt Tintsman** was born on 29 Dec 1838 in Westmoreland County, Pennsylvania, died on 31 Jul 1941 in Greensburg, Westmoreland County, Pennsylvania at age 102, and was buried in Saint Clair Cemetery.

Fifth Generation (2nd Great-Grandchildren)

111. Anna Overholt Tintsman *(John [4], John [3], Adam [2], Matthias [1])* was born on 29
Dec 1838 in Westmoreland County, Pennsylvania, died on 31 Jul 1941 in Greensburg, Westmoreland
County, Pennsylvania at age 102, and was buried in Saint Clair Cemetery.

Anna Overholt Tintsman

Research Notes: GREENSBURG'S OLDEST WOMAN IS DEAD AT AGE OF 102

GREENSBURG, July 31. - UP - The city's oldest woman, Mrs. Anna T. Leasure, 102, died
today. She was the widow of the Rev. Loren Bigelow Leasure, a Reformed Church preacher,
who held pastorates in Somerset County, Kittanning, Wilkinsburg, Emlenton and Scottsdale,
Pa., prior to his death in 1881. Mrs. Leasure, who would have been 103 years old in December,
is survived by five children, including Mrs. A. D. McGrew, Pittsburgh.

From: The News-Herald, Franklin, Pennsylvania, on Thursday July 31, 1941, Page 14

LEASURE FUNERAL SATURDAY

Funeral services for Greensburg's oldest resident, Mrs. Anna Tinstman Leasure who died at her
home in Harrison avenue at 10 o'clock Thursday morning, will be held there at 8 o'clock
Saturday afternoon. Rev. Paul Reid Pontius, D. D. minster of the Second Evangelical and Reformed Church of this city, will be
in charge of the services which will be private as will the interment following in the St. Clair cemetery. Friends are asked to omit
flowers.

From: The Greenburg Daily Tribune, Greensburg, Pennsylvania, on Friday August 1, 1941, Page 10

Correction Maiden Name: Tintsman

MRS. LEASURE CELEBRATES ROUND CENTURY OF LIVING

by Lewis C. Walkinshaw

It will come to an extremely small number of us to reach the age of 100 years, but such was the accomplishment of Mrs. Anna
Tintsman Leasure of Harrison Avenue, Greensburg. Her home was the Mecca for a host of admiring friends, relatives and
descendants. Mrs. Leasure is a descendant of Abraham Overholt, who was born in Bucks County, PA, in 1774 and came to East
Huntingdon Township at the present West Overton in 1800. Their daughter, Anna Overholt, born July 4, 1812, married John
Tintsman in 1830 who died in 1866. To this marriage were born Maria, Jacob O., Abraham O., Henry O., Anna, widow of Rev.
L. B. Leasure, John O. who died in the Civil War, Elizabeth, Emma, wife of D. W. J. K. Kline and Christian S. O. Tintsman.
Jacob Tintsman was born in Bucks County, January 13, 1773, married in Chester County December 11, 1708 to Anna Fox who
was born in Chester County August 8, 1779. Ten children were born to this marriage, and among them John Tintsman, born
January 29, 1807, in East Huntingdon Township where he lived as a respected farmer. Anna Fox Tintsman died in 1877.

The husband of the centenarian, Rev. Loren Bigelow Leasure, was a son of Abraham and Barbara (Lobingier) Leasure and was
born near Madison on October 26, 1828. He was married to Anna Tintsman November 26, 1855 and became the father of eight
children. He was licensed to preach by the quarterly conference of the United Brethren Church on January 30, 1852 and was
ordained by the annual conference at Liverpool, Perry County January 4, 1862. He changed his denominational affiliations and
was received into the Westmoreland Classes of the Reformed Church in 1868, serving pastorates in Somerset County,
Kittanning, Emlenton, Wilkinsburg and Scottdale. He died November 9, 1881 at the age of 55 years.

Mrs. Leasure's late husband came of the distinctive pioneer stock of Phillip Heck, a member of Captain Casper Walthour's
Company in the Fort Walthour settlement. One of Phillip Heck's daughters married Walthour, another Fisher, a third Garvin and
a fourth Leasure. So that, good neighbor and friend, has brought into her life the stability of pioneer Americanism, good health
and a sunny disposition.

It was a great pleasure to have her break a rule of 25 or more years' standing--not to have her picture taken and to gracefully
pose for a characteristic likeness yesterday. In doing this she accredited to the desire of her many friends and children. In the
course of the conversation, the Battle of Gettysburg was referred to. We told her how the late Hugh W. Walkinshaw, then a lad
of 13 years at Saltsburg and the late Isaac Sherrick, picking wheat sheaves in his uncle's (Peter Sherrick) wheat field near West

Overton, both declared that they hear the cannonading at Gettysburg on that eventful July day in 1863. Mrs. Leasure quickly retorted that she heard it, too. Her memory was keen enough to recall many other incidents through the years.

All honor to Greensburg's lovely lady, who has now entered the second century of a busy and happy life. Her friends and family heaped upon her many birthday cards, bouquets of beautiful flowers and other gifts and thus helped her to enjoy one of the happiest days of her life, as she was glad to express it.

Anna married **Rev. Loren Bigelow Leasure,** son of **Abraham Leasure** and **Barbara Anna Lobingier,** on 26 Nov 1855. Loren was born on 26 Oct 1826 in Madison, Westmoreland County, Pennsylvania, died on 9 Nov 1881 in Greensburg, Westmoreland County, Pennsylvania at age 55, and was buried in Saint Clair Cemetery.

(Duplicate Line. See Person 92 on Page 63)

First Generation

112. Martin Oberholtzer was born in 1709 in Frankfurt-am-Main, Heiliges Römisches Reich Deutscher Nation and died on 5 Nov 1744 in Deep Run, Bedminster Township, Bucks County, Pennsylvania at age 35.

Research Notes: Martin Overholt, born in the Rhenish Palatinate in 1709, was one of the thousands who were compelled by religious persecutions and the virulence of Franco-German warfare to forsake their native land in the

early part of the 18th century. The exact date of his arrival is not known, but it must have occurred soon after his majority in 1730. That he accompanied his fellow refugees to the recognized meeting place, at Germantown, may be safely assumed. But presently he passed on to Bucks County on the Delaware, acquired a farm apparently by lease, in Bedminster Township, married in 1736, died in 1744, in his 36th year, and was buried in the Mennonite Graveyard, leaving a son, Henry, born in 1739.

682. Martin Oberholtzer, born 1709 in Germany; died April 05, 1744. He married 683. Agnes Kolb November 02, 1736.

683. Agnes Kolb, born April 18, 1713; died February 02, 1786. She was the daughter of 1366. Henry Kolb and 1367. Barbara ? Fretz.

Children of Martin Oberholtzer and Agnes Kolb are:

i. Martin Oberholtzer

ii. John Oberholtzer

iii. Maria Oberholtzer

341 iv. Barbara Oberholtzer, born November 20, 1737; died May 08, 1823 in Bedminster, Bucks Co., PA; married Christian Fretz 1757.

v. Henry Oberholtzer, born February 05, 1738/39; died December 05, 1813; married Anna Butler January 03, 1765.

Lots of good information about the Overholts in Germany here: http://www.karensbranches.com/OberholtzerSites/Germany.html

NOTE: The discussion below credited to Betty May contains information culled from the 1903 work of Rev. A.J. Fretz titled "A Genealogical Record of the Descendants of Martin Oberholtzer: Together with Historical and Biographical Sketches and Illustrated with Portraits and Other Illustrations." (Milton, N.J.: The Press of Evergreen News, 1903).

Please also note that the Martin in the top paragraph of the the information below is the father of the Martin Jr in the second paragraph below. It is thought that Martin Sr's headstone (shown here) is a modern replacement for an earlier stone where the name of "Oberholtzer" was used (the surname being changed to the more commonly used and 'Americanized' version for various reasons). The discussion of Martin Jr outlines reasons for this change. ~ Updated by Carl Christensen October 2011.

Martin Oberholtzer (Overholt) Date of Birth 1709 at Frankfort-on-the-main (Now known as Frankfort) Germany. Married Agnes (Maiden Name unknown) on November 2, 1736. She was born April 18, 1713. They were married only eight years and had five children before his death on April 5, 1744 One child died in infancy. The four remaining children were: Barbara, Henry, Marie and Martin Jr. Agnes married a second time to William Nash and was his third wife. They had four more children. He died in 1760. Agnes died February 15, 1786 and is buried in the same cemetery where Martin is buried. Deep Run Mennonite Cemetery East.

Martin Oberholtzer Jr. and other family members changed their last name to the more English version of the name, Overholt. He was born December 20, 1743 in Bucks Co., PA. He married Esther Fretz in 1770. She was the daughter of Christian Fretz who had come to this country around 1720 along with two brothers from Baden, Germany. Martin and Esther had four children by the time the Revolutionary War broke out and fled to Canada for protection. They did not like the cold winters in Canada and moved back to Bucks Co. PA when the war was over. In 1810 Martin traveled to Ohio and purchased land in Coshocton and Tuscarawas Countied intending to move his large family (He now had forteen children) to Ohio. About six weeks before they were to make the move, he bled to death from a cancer on the neck. Esther took her large family and moved to Tuscarawas Co. Ohio.

Descendants of Martin Oberholtzer

Information supplied by Betty May (Overholt descendent)

Martin Oberholtzer's father was Marcus "Mark" Oberholtzer of 1664 to 1726.

Children of Martin Oberholtzer ("senior") are: Barbara Heinrich (aka Henry)- see link below Maria John Martin, Jr

Aug 30, 2016 7:41 PM - Findagrave User #47484531 claims that Martin's birth date is April 5, 1709 but provides no source for this information.

NOTE: That while the general area that Martin is to have emigrated from is now known as Germany, in the early 1700s, it was still a hodgepodge of Principalities that did not always have a common government. So noting his birth as 'Germany' is problematic.
See Deep Run East Mennonite East Cemetery notes about the differences between each cemetery at 'Deep Run'

Martin married **Agnes Fretz**. Agnes was born in 1713 and died in 1788 at age 75.

The child from this marriage was:
+ 113　M　　i.　**Heinrich Oberholtzer** was born on 5 Feb 1739 in Bucks County, Pennsylvania and died on 5 Mar 1813 in Westmoreland County, Pennsylvania at age 74.

Second Generation (Children)

113.　Heinrich Oberholtzer *(Martin [1])* was born on 5 Feb 1739 in Bucks County, Pennsylvania and died on 5 Mar 1813 in Westmoreland County, Pennsylvania at age 74.

Heinrich married **Anna Beitler**. Anna was born on 24 Mar 1745 in Bucks County, Pennsylvania and died on 5 Apr 1835 in Westmoreland County, Pennsylvania at age 90.

The child from this marriage was:
+ 114　M　　i.　**Abraham Overholt** was born on 19 Apr 1784 in Bucks County, Pennsylvania and died on 15 Jan 1870 in East Huntingdon twp, Westmoreland County, Pennsylvania at age 85.

Third Generation (Grandchildren)

114.　Abraham Overholt *(Heinrich [2], Martin [1])* was born on 19 Apr 1784 in Bucks County, Pennsylvania and died on 15 Jan 1870 in East Huntingdon twp, Westmoreland County, Pennsylvania at age 85.

Abraham married **Maria Stauffer**. Maria was born on 13 Jul 1791 in Fayette City, Fayette, Pennsylvania and died on 1 Nov 1874 in East Huntingdon, Westmoreland County, Pennsylvania at age 83.

Children from this marriage were:

+ 115 F i. **Anna Stauffer Overholt** was born on 4 Jul 1812 in Westoverton, Pennsylvania and died on 29 Mar 1866 in Fayette City, Fayette County, Pennsylvania at age 53.

  116 M ii. **Aaron Overholt**.

+ 117 F iii. **Elizabeth Stauffer Overholt** was born on 2 Jun 1819 in Westmoreland County, Pennsylvania and died on 1 Oct 1905 in Wooster, Wayne, Ohio at age 86.

Fourth Generation (Great-Grandchildren)

115. Anna Stauffer Overholt *(Abraham [3], Heinrich [2], Martin [1])* was born on 4 Jul 1812 in Westoverton, Pennsylvania and died on 29 Mar 1866 in Fayette City, Fayette County, Pennsylvania at age 53.

Anna married **John Tintsman**, son of **John Tintsman/Dinstman** and **Frances Stauffer**. John was born on 1 Jul 1812 in Westmoreland County, Pennsylvania, died on 29 Mar 1866 in Westmoreland County, Pennsylvania at age 53, and was buried in Mount Pleasant, Westmoreland County, Pennsylvania.

(Duplicate Line. See Person 110 on Page 70)

117. Elizabeth Stauffer Overholt *(Abraham [3], Heinrich [2], Martin [1])* was born on 2 Jun 1819 in Westmoreland County, Pennsylvania and died on 1 Oct 1905 in Wooster, Wayne, Ohio at age 86.

Elizabeth married **John Wilson Frick**. John was born on 23 Feb 1822 in Adamsburg, Westmoreland, Pennsylvania and died on 31 Aug 1888 in Wooster, Wayne, Ohio at age 66.

Children from this marriage were:

118 F   i.   **Mariah Overholt Frick** was born on 9 Feb 1848 in West Newton, Westmoreland, Pennsylvania and died on 24 Jan 1939 in Wooster, Wayne, Ohio at age 90.

119 M   ii.   **Henry Clay Frick** was born on 19 Dec 1849 in West Overton, Westmoreland, Pennsylvania and died on 2 Dec 1919 in Manhattan, New York, New York at age 69.

120 F   iii.   **Anna Overholt Frick** was born on 21 Aug 1852 in West Newton, Westmoreland, Pennsylvania and died on 9 Jun 1916 in West Newton, Westmoreland, Pennsylvania at age 63.

121 M   iv.   **Aaron Overholt Frick** was born on 7 Apr 1855 in West Newton, Westmoreland, Pennsylvania and died on 13 Oct 1922 in Stark County, Ohio at age 67.

122 M v. **Jay Edgar Frick** was born on 16 Feb 1859 in West Newton, Westmoreland, Pennsylvania and died on 28 Feb 1932 in Wooster, Wayne, Ohio at age 73.

123 F vi. **Sallie Overholt Frick** was born on 21 Mar 1862 in West Newton, Westmoreland, Pennsylvania and died on 22 Nov 1944 at age 82.

Name Index

Name Index

Name Index

THE JOSEPH FENLON FAMILY
Bertha Fenlon McGrew

Joseph Patrick Fenlon, a pioneer and resident of Mackinac County for 55 years, came from Ireland to Canada at the age of 16 together with his parents, seven brothers, and two sisters in 1882. They first settled in Seaforth, Ontario (north and slightly west of London), where they remained for 3 years. In 1885 Joseph and apparently brothers John and Edward migrated north to Sault Ste. Marie(probably via the Canadian Pacific steamer out of Owen Sound) and thence entered the US. It is said that at first they worked the lumber camps, probably the ones operated by Smith & Hossack near Rader and the Gogomain, whence Joseph walked, following lumber company tote roads and then the Indian trail that came out near the center of what now is Hessel, at the marina. The first sight that met his eyes was that of two Indian squaws in birch bark canoes lifting nets, which were filled with jumbo whitefish of a size no longer caught. The beauties and possibilities of the location so impressed him that, there and then he decided to settle near the spot. He must have returned to the Gogomain to lumber through the winter and then come back, with his brothers, in the spring. For in April of 1886 John and Edward filed side-by-side homesteads behind the Wendell owned shorefront and immediately north of those filed the previous year by Frank Pillman and David Stuart. Joseph filed for his in September north and slightly west of Mackinac Bay, behind the Wendells and George Andrews. Joseph first clerked for the Hessel family in their store, but in 1891 he and his younger brother James, it seems that by now the rest of the family had arrived, built a general store on the Hessel site of what is now the James Bowlby residence. Hessel Restaurant. This was a very traditional country store, though it later became principally a market, dealing in greengroceries, produce, meat, and general merchandise, from basic hardwares, to fabrics to toys. This burned and rebuilt in 1908, operated as The Fenlon Brothers Stores until 1950, when it was first leased, then sold to Forrest B. Dick Church of Cedarville by Hintz Fenlon, Josephs son and heir to the store. Besides Hintz, Joseph had two daughter, Ellen (Mrs. Paul Tobin) later of Akron Ohio and Bertha (Mrs. Albert D. McGrew) of Franklin, Pennsylvania. (This is who Longs bought it from in October 1986) Unable to obtain land in Ireland as a Roman Catholic under English Protestant rule, Joseph was obsessed with the acquisition of property-as his means would permit. He thus often attended and invested at tax sales. As land was acquired with suitable timber on it, the Fenlon brothers engaged in the lumber business together with their retail trade enterprise, the one business complementing the other. James died at the age of 35 and was buried on the homestead where his parents could see his grave from the window of their home. Many of the Fenlon descendants are now buried there. The township eventually took over the burial ground, but it is still the Fenlon Cemetery. Joseph died in 1940 at age 74. Both Joseph and his son, Hintz, became fluent in the Chippewa language so that they could easily communicate with the local Indians, of whom there were a goodly number through the early days of this century. In 1907 or 08 Joseph, Hintz and Bertha were inducted into the local Chippwea band with appropriate ceremonies. A great feast was held at Chief Sabtigos home, the war dance was danced, and then the pipe of peace was smoked by all. The pipe was a beautiful article, its stem was covered with Indian symbols and the bowl was of red clay inclaid with pewter. Joseph was declared Chief of the White Men and given the name Ossowanimikee, which means Yellow Thunder. Hintz was Wasagesic and Bertha, Wasagesic go quay. Bertha now of McAllen Texas still used the old family home as a summer residence. The house was built in 1897 by Joseph Kramen, boat builder and part time carpenter, without benefit of either plumb bob or square.

Written by Albert D. McGrew

STATE OF MICHIGAN
DEPARTMENT OF NATURAL RESOURCES
MACKINAC ISLAND STATE PARK COMMISSION

DONATION RECEIPT

Date Received October 14, 1982   Accession No. _______________

Received from: Mr. Albert D. McGrew _______________________________

                 Hessel, MI 49745 _________________________________

Item No.   Description

Chippewa Indian Tribal Peace Pipe. Given to Mr. Joseph

Fenlon (Grandfather of Mr. McGrew) by Chief Santigo when

Mr. Fenlon was taken into the tribe and designated as

Chief of the White Man.

This peace pipe is given by Mr. McGrew in memory of Joseph

Fenlon. The pipe will be independently appraised and a copy

of the appraisal will be sent to Mr. McGrew.

Phil Porter, Historian
Mackinac Island State Park Comm.
Box 370
Mackinac Island, MI
    49757

The objects described above have been received by the Mackinac Island State Park
Commission as a gift, and the owner or his agent with full authority desiring to
absolutely transfer full title by signing below, hereby gives, assigns and con-
veys, finally and completely, and without any limitation, condition, or reserva-
tion, the property described above to the Mackinac Island State Park Commission,
its successors and assigns, permanently and forever, together with (when appli-
cable) any copyrights therein and the right to hereafter copyright the same.

Accepted for the Commission: Owner's or agent's signature:

_______________________________   _______________________________
Phil Porter, Historian

RICHARD A. POHRT
1407 W PATERSON
FLINT, MICHIGAN 48504
1-313-238-2569

January 24, 1983

Mr. David A. Armour
Mackinac Island State
Park Commission
P.O. Box 30028
Lansing, Michigan 48909

Dear Mr. Armour:

I have carefully reviewed the photographs of the two American
Indian pipes recently donated to the Mackinac Island State Park
Commission. It is my opinion that both are Chippewa, and esti-
mate they were made in the second half of the 19th Century. A
good date would be C-1860.

1. Catlinite bowl with lead inlay. Short ash wood stem
    with some branding with a hot file. Value $300.00

2. Small Catlinite L-shape bowl. Long (27 inch) ash wood
    stem decorated with perforations and branded with a
    hot file or rasp. Value $350.00

Sincerely,

Richard A. Pohrt

RAP:cj

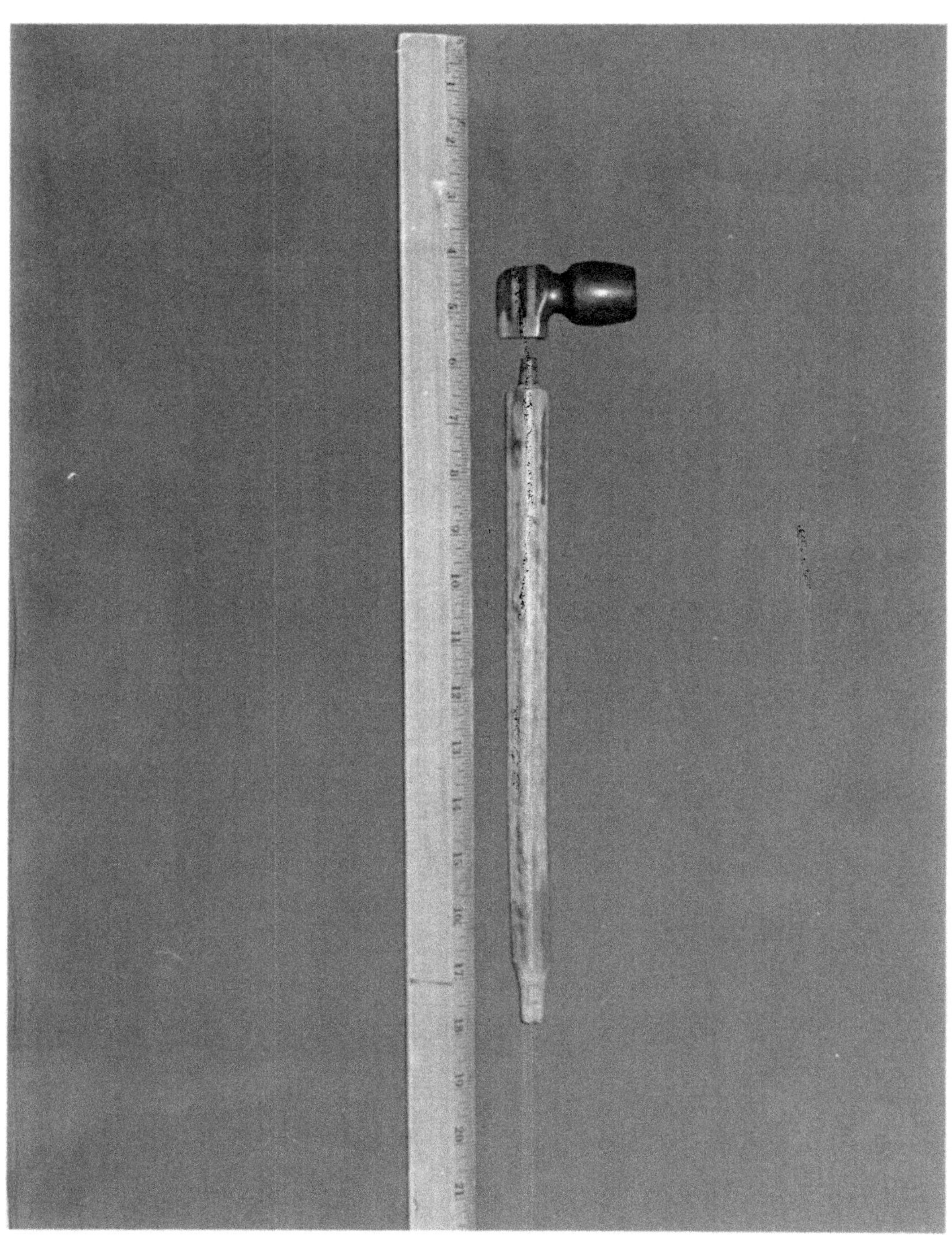

Fenlon Peace Pipe

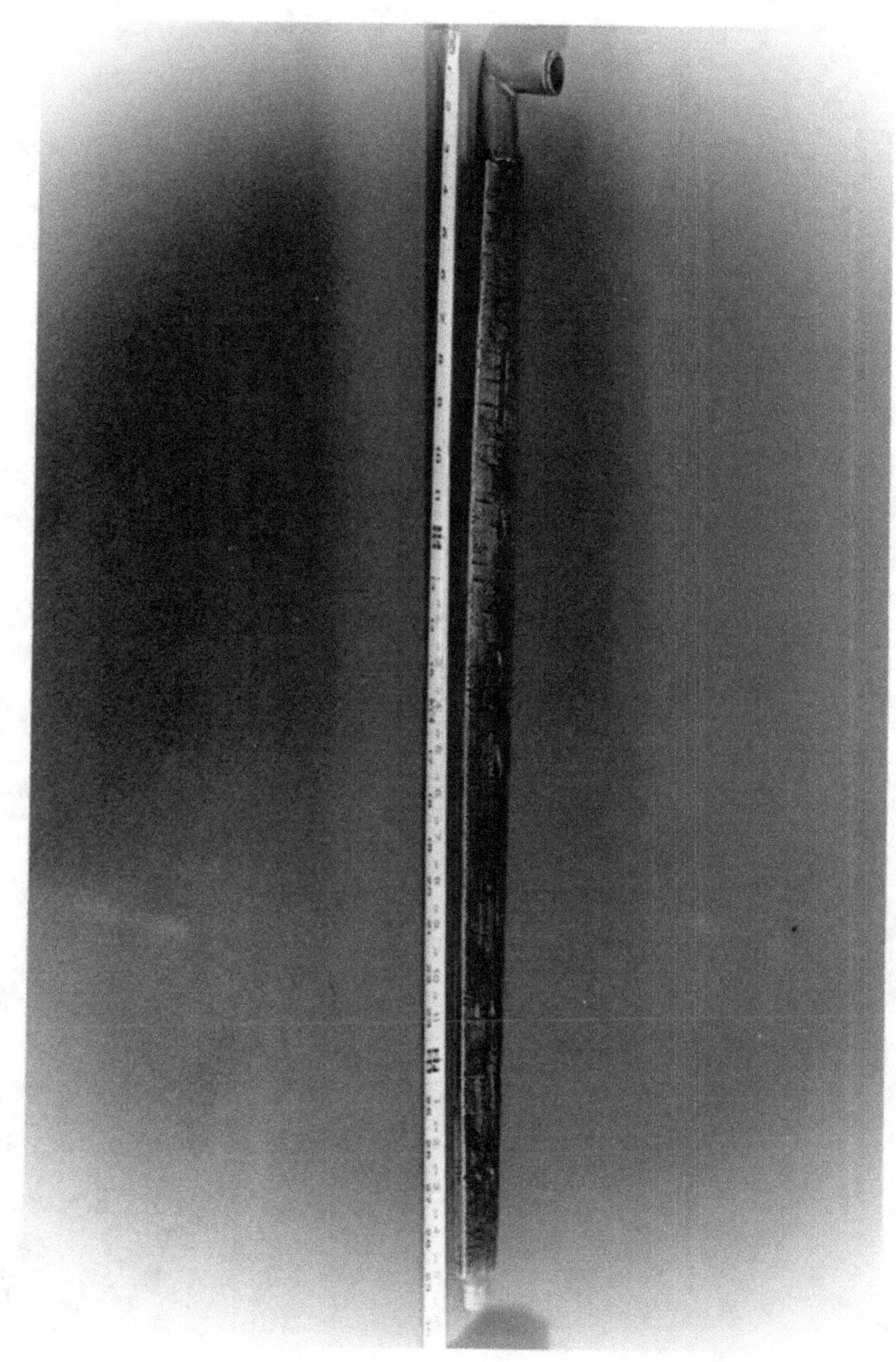

Fenlon Peacepipe2

Frick and Overholt whiskey homestead marks bicentennial

By David Clucas
FOR THE TRIBUNE-REVIEW

Rodney Sturtz, executive director of West Overton Museums in East Huntingdon Township, poses for a photo in Abraham Overholt's room on the grounds.

West Overton is celebrating its 200th anniversary this year.

Eric McCandless/Tribune-Review

Two hundred years ago, 30 wagons carried Henry Overholt and his entire family to East Huntington Township near Scottdale.

The community they established, West Overton, went on to serve as the origin of a successful whiskey business and the birthplace of Henry Clay Frick.

This year, West Overton Museums plan to celebrate the bicentennial anniversary of the village. Executive Director Rodney Sturtz said the celebration will begin in April, when Overholt originally signed the deed for the property two centuries ago.

Overholt was a farmer and weaver. In 1859, his son, Abraham, opened a distillery where he produced "Old Overholt" and "Old Farm" whiskeys. The business turned highly profitable, with Overholt whiskey sold worldwide.

Frick was born in 1849. Frick's father, John, worked in the distillery and married Abraham's daughter, Elizabeth. H.C. Frick went on to become a millionaire in the coke business and later worked with steel tycoon Andrew Carnegie.

Two buildings in West Overton have stood for 200 years.

In 1800, Overholt built the Spring House with 18-inch-thick stone walls to serve as a central pool for three springs in the surrounding hills. "They dug trenches, put in clay pipe and diverted the water from those springs to the Spring House," Sturtz said.

The Spring House, now on the National Register of Historic Places, still works, with its pool of ice-cold water measuring from 11 to 14 inches, according to Sturtz.

The Overholts also used the pool to preserve foods such as eggs and vegetables.

Also still functional is the 200-year-old Smoke House, where the Overholts hung ham and venison on metal hooks and a fire in the middle of the room would smoke the meats.

It has become a highlight on tours for elementary school students. "We just wait for the question," Sturtz said. "Because some brave kid always asks, 'Does that mean this is where you would have to come if you wanted to smoke?'"

Both buildings are in good condition for their ages, according to Sturtz. Several years ago, each roof was painstakingly rebuilt with historical accuracy.

Celebration

West Overton Museums in East Huntingdon Township will sponsor a series of events commemorating its bicentennial.

▶ April 14 — A 200th anniversary dinner at the museums. Guest speaker is Martha Sanger, great-granddaughter of Henry Clay Frick. Tickets are $25.

▶ May 2 — 2000 season opens to the public. Tours are available. Cost is $5 for adults, $3 for senior citizens and $2 for children 12 and under.

▶ May 30-July 16 — The annual West Overton Quilt Show featuring national and regional quilts.

▶ Sometime in June — A performance by the Pittsburgh Opera at the West Overton barn.

▶ July 22 — Annual garden tour through Mt. Pleasant and Scottdale.

▶ Aug. 5-6 — Civil War Living History Weekend sponsored by the West Overton Sons of Union Veterans. Visit the Civil War soldiers as they camp on the museum grounds. Special exhibits and programs will be held all weekend.

Museum hours are 10 a.m.-4 p.m. Tuesday through Saturday and 1-5 p.m. Sundays. For more information, call the museum at (724) 887-7910.

TRIB LIVE

Old whiskey bottles are among the items on display at West Overton Village and Museums in Scottdale.

The West Overton Village and Museums is on Route 819 between Route 119 and Scottdale in East Huntingdon.

According to Jessica Kadie-Barclay, museums managing director, and Stephanie Koller, registrar, a group of Mennonites led by Henry Overholt crossed the Alleghenies from eastern Pennsylvania and established a farming settlement they called West Overton.

Overholt became known for distilling spirits from local grains. But before becoming distillers, Abraham Overholt's nephew, Henry Overholt Overholt, weaved coverlets for sale. Abraham Overholt, then 16, came with his father to the settlement in 1802. Abraham and his brother, Christian, had begun the distillery, processing grains from the farm.

Abraham bought out Christian's share and began to develop the farm's resources, building the three-story brick house and later the distillery "At some point between 1818 and 1828, he decided it was profitable to keep expanding the distillery operations," said Kadie-Barclay.

In those days, the best way to ship farm grains to the eastern markets was to distill them into whiskey for shipment. "Whiskey was also used as currency and a medicine," said Koller.

"People traded whiskey for what they needed." Farmers took their grains to Overholt to be ground and fermented. In exchange, Overholt kept a portion of the whiskey.

DISTILLERY OPERATIONS

The distillery began with one still, but by 1829, Overholt had four stills in operation.

By 1838, he had combined two operations — milling the grains with fermenting the spirits — into one operation. Before that time, he had sent the grains to a mill to be processed into flour, requiring transportation to a mill and back. By combining the operation in one place — in the six-story building Abraham Overholt built across from the house — he was able to beat his competition, according to Koller.

In time, Old Farm, a pure rye whiskey, became known around the world. A second distillery was built near Connellsville at Broadford.

FAMILY TREE

Abraham Overholt's daughter, Elizabeth, married John Frick, a laborer. In 1849, they had a son, Henry Clay Frick, who was born in the springhouse at West Overton.

According to Kadie-Barclay, the young Frick was not a robust child. He was doted on by his mother and grandmother. He learned business and bookkeeping in the companies owned by his grandfather and an uncle in Mt. Pleasant.The young Frick developed a strong sense of how to make money. While working at the Broadford distillery, he learned of the vast coal resources in the region around Scottdale and Connellsville. He began to buy the rights to the coal.

He had coke ovens built and bought shares in the Mt. Pleasant & Broadford Railroad. Later, he was able to make a healthy profit by selling the railroad to B&O Railroad.

In addition to Old Farm, Old Overholt whiskey was distilled.

Frick died in 1919 at the beginning of prohibition and the distillery at West Overton closed.

ABOUT H.C. FRICK

Many people in the area believe Frick was a villain.

Cassandra Vivian, volunteer curator at the Mt. Pleasant Glass Museum, said Frick provided better pay and working conditions than most other business owners, and he developed the industries that supported the people who lived in communities like Scottdale and Mt. Pleasant.

Frick funded many things for his workers, building baseball fields, providing uniforms and constructing swimming pools. "One of the most important things to remember about Frick is the time in which he was an active businessman," Koller said. "By today's standards, yes he was terrible, but in that day, asking someone to work 16 hours in a mine wasn't far from the norm.

"Aside from Johnstown (1889 Johnstown Flood), much of what he is remembered for is Homestead (an 1892 labor strike at the Homestead Works of the Carnegie Steel Company). He was actually Carnegie's scapegoat. Also, unlike Carnegie, Rockefeller, Vanderbilt, etc., much of Frick's charity work was done anonymously and without the pomp and circumstance."

Frick is blamed for the problems that caused the dam at the millionaire's resort above Johnstown to burst, killing many residents in that city in the resulting flood in 1889. He also is blamed for the labor strike that resulted in nine workers being killed and 70 injured.

OLD OVERHOLT MEDICINE

During prohibition, Old Overholt, distilled in Broadford, continued to be produced as medicine that was available by prescription. Production of Old Overholt moved to Cincinnati, then to Kentucky, where it is still distilled by Jim Beam.

Aaron Overholt, who married Frick's sister, Mariah, moved into the house at West Overton. They lived there until 1922, when Frick's daughter, Helen, who inherited a large sum of money from her father, purchased the buildings over a period of time and turned them into a museum.

In 1943, West Overton became independent. Plans to expand operations at West Overton are in the works. The first whiskey to be distilled since 1919 will become available this year, according to the museum website.

The whiskey will be distilled from rye grown on the property or raised on local farms, Koller said. The whiskey will be available in the fall, and a whiskey festival will be held in October. Visitors will be able to taste and purchase the product.

The West Overton Village and Museums is at 109 West Overton Road in Scottdale. Tours of the house, summer kitchen and springhouse, where Frick was born, are offered during the summer. Call the museum at 724-887-7910 or check the website for details.

Karl Polacek is a staff writer for Trib Total Media. He can be reached

---

N AN EARLY SUMMER DAY in 1800, there was great excitement at the Overholt farm in Bucks County on the Delaware River. Henry and Anna Overholt were at last starting on the adventure they had been dreaming about since the end of the Revolutionary War.

Sitting around the campfires at night, soldiers from Westmoreland County who had crossed the mountains to fight with Gen. Anthony Wayne had told how rich the Youghiogheny valley was. Henry listened to these tales and resolved to head for the western part of the state.

But he was 61 and Anna 55 before they finally sold their Bucks County farm and loaded up the covered wagons for the perilous trip over the Pennsylvania mountains.

Buried in the Mennonite graveyard in Bucks County were Henry's parents who had fled persecution in the Palatinate on the Rhine and had come to America in 1732.

Five sons, six daughters, five sons-in-law, two daughters-in-law, 13 grandchildren—33 in all climbed into the wagons and started off on the 300-mile journey. The sizable caravan creaked over the rutted roads, forded the swollen streams and came at last to the rolling country of southwestern Pennsylvania.

Land was cheap, well-wooded and pleasantly patched with emerald meadows. The senior Overholts selected a hilltop in what was later to become West Overton and there built an imposing home which still stands. The rest of the family settled down on nearby farms.

At the deaths of Henry and Anna Overholt, their son Abraham inherited the farm. An enterprising and respected man, Abraham Overholt had the further distinction of being the maternal grandfather of Henry Clay Frick.

The West Overton home of the Abraham Overholts

On a portion of the farm which Abraham purchased from his brother Christian was a small log distillery which formed the nucleus for the production of Overholt whiskey and brought the largest fortune in the area to its owners.

Abraham Overholt served another and far more important office in the industrial history of the nation. He discovered the coal that was later mined and baked by his grandson into coke which indirectly produced some of the greatest fortunes in America.

But the Overholt stamp was left on Henry Clay Frick in another and more personal way. Tall, courtly Abraham Overholt, a staunch Mennonite, was an industrious man of strong principle and tremendous energy. In his black broadcloth suit and wide-brimmed silk hat, he was a distinguished figure who commanded the respect and admiration of the community.

Equally imposing was Abraham's wife, Maria Stauffer, dressed exquisitely in her black or ashes of roses cashmere and her cap of bobbinet lace, her velvet-trimmed silk capes.

A UNIQUE CELEBRATION IN THE M'GREW FAMILY

Seventieth Birthday Anniversary of Husband and Sixty-Fifth of Wife Observed On Same Day—Historic Family Lineage

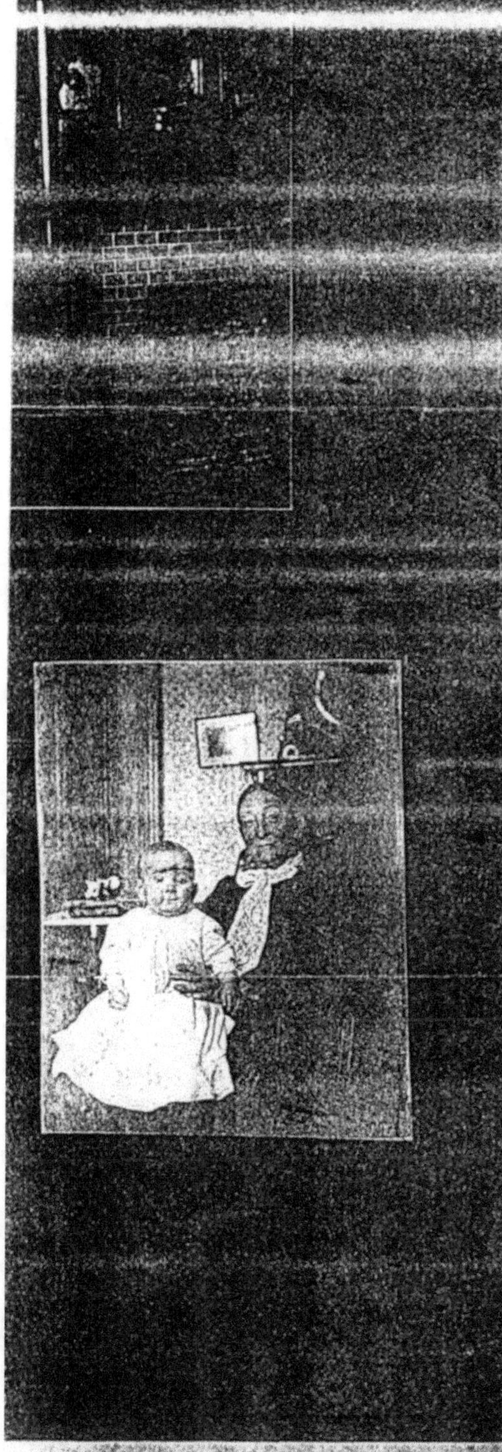

On Thursday last at the new home of Dr. W. E. McGrew, corner Broad and Graham streets, East End, was quietly celebrated an event of more than passing interest. The occasion was the dinner in honor of the seventieth anniversary of the birth of B. G. McGrew and the sixty-fifth of his wife, they both being born on the same day of the month. Another unusual fact was commented on that day. Mr. McGrew has eight children and 29 grandchildren, and the Grim Reaper has never yet called upon him to mourn the death of child or grandchild.

Benjamin Gilbert McGrew can trace his ancestry back to the famous Rob Roy McGregor, of Scotland. From thence the family was driven to the North of Ireland on account of religious persecution, where the name was shortened to McGrew.

The next positively known facts in regard to the ancestry are that in 1683, in the County of Cornwall, in the West of England "for his faithfulness in attending religious meetings of the people called Quakers, he was imprisoned in Launceston jail for some time."

Emigrating to America with the colony founded by William Penn, in 1682 or soon after, it is known that his ancestor, John Gilbert, purchased 600 acres of land at Byberry, near Philadelphia, December 19, 1695. In 1711 Benjamin Gilbert, great-grandfather of B. G. McGrew, was born at Byberry.

Little more is known of the family until 1780, when Benjamin Gilbert, with his family and one or two others, in all 15 people, were captured by the Indians known as the Five Nations, and compelled to walk from near Philadelphia to Niagara Falls, where the British then had a fort.

After incredible hardships, the entire family were finally ransomed or otherwise released, through the efforts of the British officers. With the exception of the father of the family, who died on the voyage down the St. Lawrence river to Montreal, all finally reached their Quaker friends near their former home, which the Indians had burned, not far from Philadelphia, during the year 1782. Among these captives was Abner Gilbert, the grandfather of B. G. McGrew.

Abner Gilbert located in Sewickley township, Westmoreland county, Pa., shortly after the year 1800, where his son, Benjamin Gilbert, and daughter, Susannah, the latter the mother of B. G. McGrew, were born. B. G. McGrew was born in Sewickley township, Westmoreland county March 31, 1834. His father, A. B. McGrew, was one of the early county treasurers of the county.

In early life Mr. McGrew was a school teacher, as was his wife, then Catherine Howell, of near Turtle Creek, Pa., known as "The Belle of the Turnpike," an account of her beauty. They were married November 1, 1857, and have the following children: Mrs. J. P. Douglass, wife of a prominent farmer of Westmoreland county; John F., a painter; A. B. and W. C., of the Keystone Security and Investment Co. of this city; D. G., with the Columbia Graphite Co., of Crown Point Center, New York; Mrs. F. B. Adams, wife of the Wheeling, W. Va., stock broker; Dr. W. E., and Sara, at home with her parents, on North St. Clair street, East End.

Mrs. McGrew's grandfather fought in the Revolutionary War with General George Washington, and was with the troops at Valley Forge during that memorable winter when the rations consisted of a gill of rice a day, and the footprints of the men on the snow were marked by the blood from the feet of the men, because the government could not afford to buy shoes for its troops. Mrs. McGrew's ancestors were the French Huguenots, who left France on account of religious persecution.

B. G. McGrew, for almost half a century, was a factor in the commercial life of Western Pennsylvania. At different times during his business career he was a merchant, a coal operator, a leading oil broker, finally ending his active business life as cashier of the United States pension office in this city, which position he resigned in 1899, since which time he has lived in retirement.

During the Civil War he served his country as lieutenant in a Pennsylvania regiment until compelled to resign on account of disabilities. Unassuming, quiet, generous to a fault, Mr. McGrew probably has not an enemy on earth.

McGrew celebrates 100th birthday with family

From staff reports

Albert D. McGrew, a resident of Camlu Care Center since Oct. 1997, celebrated his 100th birthday with family, friends, staff and residents.

McGrew was born in Pittsburgh, Pa., on Jan. 22, 1898, the sixth of seven children of Minnie L. and A.B. McGrew. He attended local schools, and from the age of eight, pursued a lifelong interest in ornithology, that took him all over the world.

He attended Penn State University where he was a member of Phi Gamma Delta fraternity. He left Penn State to enlist in the Air Corps and became a pilot during World War I, though the war ended before he saw overseas duty. His piloting the famous "Flying Jenney" left him with a permanent hearing loss in one ear.

After the war, he returned to finish college at the University of Washington, where he graduated with the first class of seven men to receive a logging engineering degree in the nation.

He was a logging engineer with the firm of Wheeler and Dusinberre in western Pennsylvania, and later became an independent distributor for Socony Vac-

See McGREW, 4C

Al McGrew turned 100 years old in Camlu Thursday. Standing behind him are children, from left, Anne and Natalie McGrew, Mary Mcgrew Brewer and Chuck Brewer. McGrew was born in Pittsburgh, Pa. in 1898, and was a Rio Grande Valley resident in McAllen for some 40 years. (Times photo by Ken Schmidt)

uum (now Mobil) establishing, buying and distributing to service stations in that area. He resided in Franklin, Pa. with his wife Bertha, and three daughters, for 40 years.

While in Franklin, he was an active Mason, a charter member of the Franklin Club, and Wanango Country Club and a co-owner of the CP Golf Course and other properties.

He taught logging engineering at the University of Georgia, and during World War II, taught celestial navigation for Cornell University, while a member of the U.S. Coast Guard, patrolling Lake Erie during the war.

His love of birds brought him to the Rio Grande Valley of Texas, where he was an active ornithologist, giving his outstanding pictures of many varieties of birds – taken from nesting through hatching in all the bird sanctuaries of South Texas — to the University of Texas, Pan Am. in Edinburg. At one time, he was given his own key to the then young Santa Ana Refuge.

McGrew has been a member of the Ancient Accepted Scottish Rite Northern Masonic Jurisdiction of Freemasonry No. 32 since 1918.

His daughters, Anne McGrew of Walnut Creek, Calif., and Natalie McGrew of Canton, Ohio, flew in to celebrate the occasion. His daughter, Mary and son-in-law Buck Brewer, were blessed by his presence with them in their home, since the death of his wife of 69 years in 1993, until his move into assisted living in late June 1997, then to Camlu Care Center in October, following a fractured hip. Six grandchildren and five great-grandchildren recall their "Grumpy" with deep affection.

Generations after Albert Douthett McGrew first wore this Baptismal gown in 1898. His children Anne Leasure McGrew (1926), Natalie Jane McGrew (1929), Mary Fenlon McGrew (1934) wore it. Natalie's children were next: William Albert Jaeck (1953), Shawna Marie Jaeck (1954), and Kathleen Elizabeth Jaeck (1953). Shawna's children Erika Marie Hunt (1982) and Jason Warren Hunt (1986) wore it. Finally, Erika's children Evelyn Marie Hasford (2017) and Clara Hope Hasford (2019)carried on the tradition, and the gown continues to be passed on.

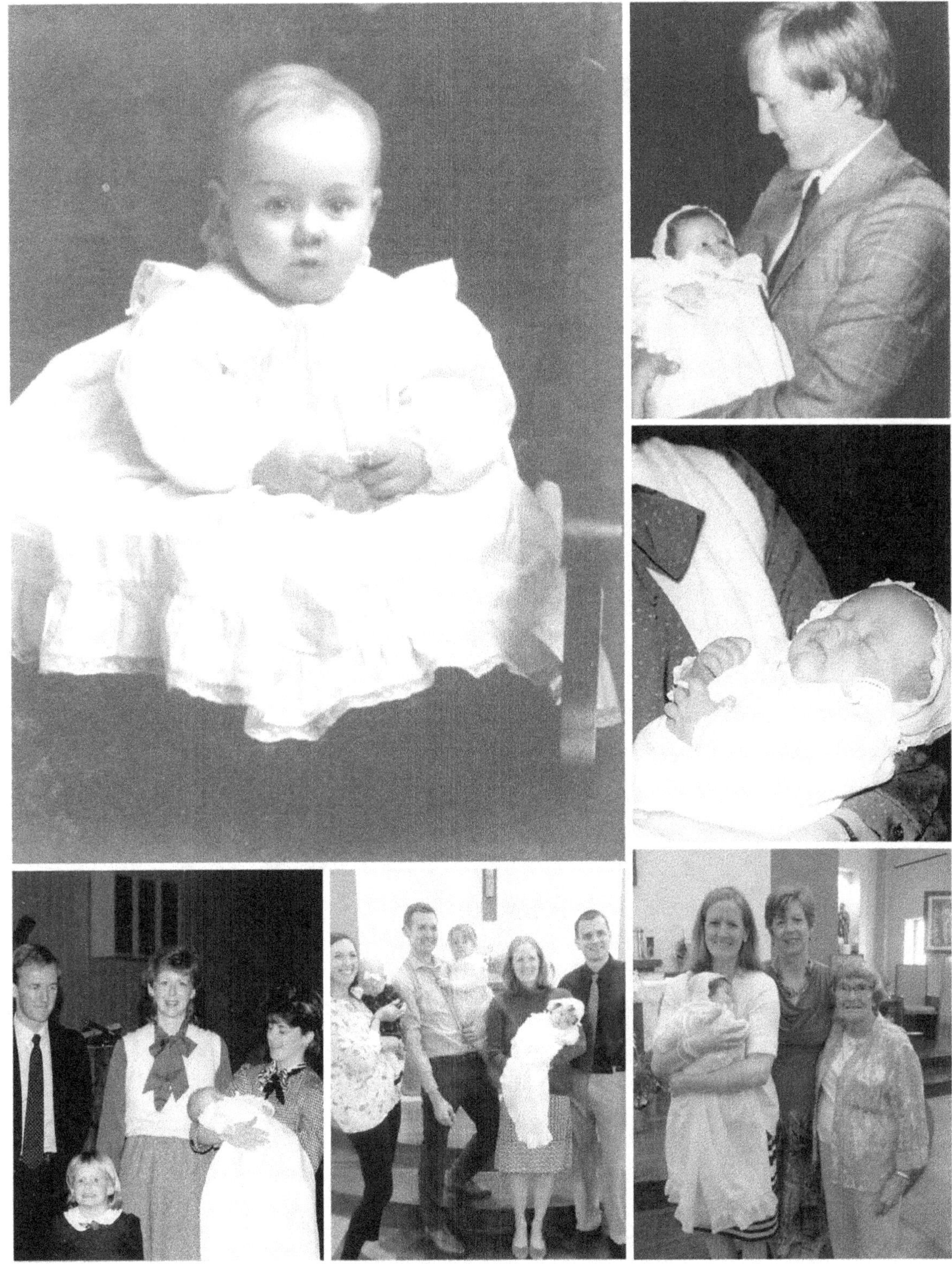

Application of NATALIE JANE McGREW ____   *DAR Research*

from: THE McGREW FAMILY, taken also from THE BOYD FAMILY, by
         Scott Lee Boyd, Govt. Printing office, 1933

A.F — another proof of births, deaths, marriages *of*

✓ Benjamin Gilbert McGrew   Katherine Rowash Howell

        b. March 31,1834   b. March 31,1839
        d. August 3,1904   d. January 8,1910

                         m. November 17,1857

                Children of Benjamin and Katherine McGrew

    Minerva Etta McGrew   John Pollock Douglass
        b. September 9,1858   b. April 20,1856
        d. December 9,1927   d. August 1,1934

                         m. February 1,1881

    John Franklin McGrew
        b.   1859
        d. May 20,1910

    Archibald B. McGrew   Minnie Leasure
        b. March 29,1861   b. January 21,1864
        d. April 14,1919   d. June 28,1952

                         m. October 23,1883

    Dilwyn Gilbert McGrew
        b. September 14,1864
        d. November 19,1923

    William Edgar McGrew   Carrie B. Kramer
        b.   1866
        d. January 15,1913   d. May 15,1920

                         m.

    Sarah Shirwell McGrew
        b. December 29,1867
        d. December 25,1951

    Susan Belle McGrew   Franklin Ball Adams
        b. March 7,1870   b.
        d. April 14,1937   d. November 1918

                         m. January 10, 1895

    Wesley Cope McGrew   Alma Adelaide Marian Johnson
        b. March 24,1875   b. January 13,1873
        d. March 15,1946   d. February 24,1930

                         m. April 17,1900

Benjamin G. McGrew was apparently born in Sewickley Twp., Westmoreland County,
Pa. and lived there during his youth. He was the son of Archibald B. McGrew and
Susanna Gilbert who were also married at Sewickley in 1822. The family belonged
to the Society of Friends (Quakers) and are listed as members of the Providence
Monthly meeting. When the children were married, however, they married outside
the church and were disowned. The record shows that Benjamin was disowned on the
first day of the seventh month of 1858 (after his marriage) Very little is known
about Katherine Howell but it is understood that she lived in Irwin, Pa. They
were married near Turtle Creek, Allegheny County by Jonathan Fulton.

THE NATIONAL SOCIETY OF THE

Daughters of the American Revolution

This certifies that

Natalie Jane Mc Grew Jaech

is a regularly approved member of the National Society of the Daughters of the American Revolution having been admitted by the National Board of Management by virtue of her descent from a patriot who with unfailing loyalty rendered material aid to the cause of American Independence during the Revolutionary War.

Given under our hands and the seal of the National Society this fourth day of February 1983

National No. 669937

Admitted February 4th 1983

Patricia W. Shelby
President General

Dorothy S. Williams
Recording Secretary General

Yvonne Spann Boone
Registrar General

Nat,

Thought you'd like seeing this. Sent a copy to Bill. Sort of the same style as Anne's original.

Love, Mary

Bertha Fenlon McGrew 5/1/93

Bertha Fenlon McGrew, 94, of Alpine, Texas, a former Franklin resident, died Wednesday, April 7, 1993, in Big Bend Regional Medical Center in Texas.

She was born June 9, 1898, in the family home in Hessel, Mich., in the upper peninsula of Michigan.

Mrs. McGrew had been a permanent resident of Texas for the past 30 years, residing with her husband, Albert McGrew, who survives. She also lived in McAllen, Texas, at one time.

She spent her young life in Hessel, returning every summer with her husband until 1987 when they occupied the old Fenlon family home in the middle of the village.

Mrs. McGrew was taken into the Chippewa Indian tribe with her brother, Hintz, and her father, Joseph, who was designated "Chief of the White Men." Her given Indian name was Wasagesic-go-quay which means "a lovely red sunset." She considered this one of the outstanding honors of her life.

She attended Ursiline Academy in Saint Ignace, Mich., the Soo High School in Sault Sainte Marie, Mich., Western Reserve University and The Cleveland School of Fine Arts. She graduated from Columbia University with honors and a B.A. degree in fine arts. She was asked to teach there and continue her education toward a master's degree.

However, she chose to marry her childhood sweetheart, Albert D. McGrew of Pittsburgh, who summered for many years on Goat Island in Lake Huron, Mich., and who later as a young man, worked for her father in the Fenlon General Store.

Mr. and Mrs. McGrew moved to Franklin where they spent 40 years of their married life. She served as a volunteer with the Girl Scouts for many years while her own children were growing up. They retired to McAllen, Texas, in the Rio Grande Valley where they spent 29 years before moving last April to Alpine with their daughter, Mary, and son-in-law, Charles.

Surviving are her husband; three daughters, Anne L. McGrew of Walnut Creek, Calif., Natalie J. McGrew of Canton, Ohio, and Mrs. Charles (Mary M.) Brewer of Alpine, Texas; six grandchildren; and five great-grandchildren.

Mrs. McGrew was preceded in death by her sister, Ellen, in 1992, and earlier by her brother, Hintz.

Mass of Christian Burial was celebrated in St. James Church in Alpine.

Cremation followed and the ashed will be buried in the Fenlon family cemetery with her parents, brother and many aunts, uncles and cousins.

Memorial contributions may be sent to Our Lady of the Snows Catholic Church in Hessel, Mich. 49745.

Arrangements are being handled by the Geeslin Funeral Home of Alpine, Texas, and the Reamer Funeral Home of Pickford, Mich.

Archibald B. McGrew.

Archibald B. McGrew died Monday morning of pneumonia in his home, 5611 Stanton avenue, after five days' illness. Mr. McGrew was born in Shaner Station, Pa., March 29, 1861, and had resided in Greensburg a number of years prior to coming to Pittsburgh, about 17 years ago. He had since been engaged as a financier, and gained wide prominence in the financial world of Pittsburgh as well as elsewhere. Mr. McGrew was a member of the Sixth United Presbyterian Church, the Chamber of Commerce and other organizations. He leaves his widow, Mrs. Minnie L. McGrew, four daughters, Mrs. Paul C. Lappe, Mrs. Frank J. Sands, Mrs. Edward Smythe and Miss Millie E. McGrew; three sons, Roy L., Archibald B. Jr., and Alfred D. McGrew of Pittsburgh; two brothers, D. G. McGrew of New York and W. C. McGrew of Pittsburgh, and three sisters, Miss Sarah McGrew and Mrs. John Douglass of Fresno, Cal., and Mrs. C. Adams of Los Angeles.

Clipped By:

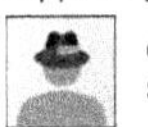

Gemma15
Sat, Apr 11, 2015

CERTIFICATE OF DEATH

Form V. S. No. 1—36M-7-13-17.

COMMONWEALTH OF PENNSYLVANIA
DEPARTMENT OF HEALTH
BUREAU OF VITAL STATISTICS

510 / 6/

V

PLACE OF DEATH.

County of *Allegheny*

Township of

Borough of

City of *Pittsburgh* (No.) 5-611 *Stanton* (St.) 11 Ward.

Registration District No.

Primary Registration District No.

File No. 41116

Registered No. 4183

[If death occurred in a Hospital or Institution, give its NAME instead of street and number.]

2. FULL NAME *Archibald B. McGrew*

PERSONAL AND STATISTICAL PARTICULARS

3. SEX *Male*

4. COLOR OR RACE *white*

5. SINGLE, MARRIED, WIDOWED OR DIVORCED (Write the word) *Married*

6. DATE OF BIRTH *March 29 1861* (Month) (Day) (Year)

7. AGE *58* yrs. X mos. *15* ds.

If LESS than 1 day, how many .... hrs. or .... min.?

8. OCCUPATION
(a) Trade, profession, or particular kind of work *Capatitist*
(b) General nature of industry, business, or establishment in which employed (or employer)

9. BIRTHPLACE (State or Country) *Pennsylvania*

10. NAME OF FATHER *Benjamin F. McGrew*

11. BIRTHPLACE OF FATHER (State or Country) *Pennsylvania*

12. MAIDEN NAME OF MOTHER *Catherine Howell*

13. BIRTHPLACE OF MOTHER (State or Country) *Pennsylvania*

14. THE ABOVE IS TRUE TO THE BEST OF MY KNOWLEDGE.

Informant *Minnie G. McGrew*

(Address) 5-611 *Stanton Ave*

21. APR 1 5 1919 *J. O. Crawford*

Filed (Legal) Registrar

MEDICAL CERTIFICATE OF DEATH

16. DATE OF DEATH *April 14 1919* (Month) (Day) (Year)

17. I HEREBY CERTIFY, That I attended deceased from *4/9* 191*9*, to *4/14* 191*9*, that I last saw h—— alive on *4/14* 191*9*, and that death occurred, on the date stated above, at *8 43* A. M.

The CAUSE OF DEATH was as follows:

Lobar Pneumonia

9 da. (Duration) yrs. mos. *5* ds.

Contributory (Secondary)

(Duration) yrs. mos. ds.

(Signed) *J. M. Lueties* M. D.

4/14 191*9* (Address) *7024 Lexley Ave*

*State the DISEASE CAUSING DEATH; or in deaths from VIOLENT CAUSES, state (1) MEANS OF INJURY; and (2) whether ACCIDENTAL, SUICIDAL, or HOMICIDAL.

18. LENGTH OF RESIDENCE (For Hospitals, Institutions, Transients or Recent Residents.)

At Place of death ..... yrs. ..... mos. ..... ds. In the State ..... yrs. ..... mos. ..... ds.

Where was disease contracted, if not at place of death?

Former or usual residence

19. PLACE OF BURIAL OR REMOVAL *Greensburg Pa*

DATE OF BURIAL *April 16 1919*

20. UNDERTAKER *Thos. B. Moreland Co.*

ADDRESS *West Stanton*

DECLARATION OF INTENTION.

THE STATE OF OHIO, } PROBATE COURT.
Franklin County, ss.

Personally Appeared in open Court _Edward Fenton_ an alien, who being duly sworn, deposes and says that he is a native of _Ireland_ that he arrived in the United States in the month of _May_ A. D. 1884, and it is bona fide his intention to become a Citizen of the United States of America, and to renounce forever, all allegiance and fidelity to any Foreign Prince, Potentate, State, or Sovereignty, and particularly to _Victoria Queen of Grd Britain & Ireland_ whose subject he is.

Edward + Fenton
his mark

Sworn to before me, and signed in my presence, this _22_ day of _June_ A. D. 1885

Charles G. Saffin
Probate Judge and ex-officio Clerk.

THE STATE OF OHIO, } PROBATE COURT.
Franklin County, ss.

BE IT REMEMBERED, That on the _22nd_ day of _June_ in the year of our Lord one thousand eight hundred and eighty _five_ personally appeared before me _Charles G. Saffin_ Judge and ex-officio Clerk of the Probate Court, within and for the County of Franklin, and State of Ohio _Edward Fenton_ an alien, a native of _Ireland_ and makes report of himself for Naturalization; who being duly sworn according to law on his oath, doth declare and say it is bona fide his intention to become a Citizen of the United States of America, and to renounce forever, all allegiance and fidelity to any Foreign Prince, Potentate, State or Sovereignty, and particularly to _Victoria Queen of Great Britain and Ireland_ whose subject he is.

ATTEST:

Charles G. Saffin
Probate Judge and ex-officio Clerk.

<No. 1>

131

[Class I comprises all persons subject to do military duty between the ages of twenty and thirty-five years, and all unmarried persons subject to do military duty above the age of thirty-five years and under the age of forty-five.   Class II comprises all other persons subject to military duty.]

SCHEDULE II.—CONSOLIDATED LIST of all persons of CLASS II, subject to do military duty in the _Twenty first_ Congressional District, consisting of the Counties of _Indiana_ _Westmoreland_ and _Fayette_ State of _Pennsylvania_, enumerated during the month of _June_ 1863 , under direction of _Capt Wm B Coulter_, Provost Marshal.

RESIDENCE			NAME	DESCRIPTION			PLACE OF BIRTH (Naming the State, Territory, or Country.)	FORMER MILITARY SERVICE	REMARKS	
				Age 1st July 1863.	White or Colored.	Profession, Occupation, or Trade.				
moreland										
awick Co	1	1	Light Elias	35	White	Hotel Keeper	Penna			1
urg Kor	2	2	Lowery William G	33	"	Horsedealer	"			2
jael 7 P	3	3	Leasure Solon B	36	"	Minister				3
"	4	4	Leasure John B	35	"	Justice Peace				4
"	5	5	Long Samuel	40	"	Hotel Keeper	"			5
"	6	6	Long John	37	"	Stone Mason	"			6
"	7	7	Long Simon	44	"	Farmer	"			7
"	8	8	Long Jacob	35	"	Carpenter	"			8
"	9	9	Long Adam	40	"	Farmer				9
"	10	10	Long Andrew	36	"	"	"			10
"	11	11	Long Daniel	37	"	"	"			11
"	12	12	Lontz David	36	"	"	"			12
"	13	13	Latimer William	39	"	"	"			13
urgingstan 18	14	14	Leighlly Eli C	43	"	Merchant	"			14
"	15	15	Lane Bennett	42	"	Farmer				15
"	16	16	Lynn James S	47	"	"	"			16
"	17	17	Lapp Henry	43	"	Laborer	"			17
"	18	18	Lunchberger Frederick	43	"	Miner	Germany			18
"	19	19	Latta Ephraim	40	"	Farmer	Penna			19
Sewickly	20	20	Lusk Asa	42	"	"	"			20

To Colonel JAMES B. FRY,
Provost Marshal General U. S.,
Washington, D. C.

STATION: _Headquarters_   Congr. Dist. of ______
DATE: ______

______ Provost Marshal.

MICHIGAN DEPARTMENT OF HEALTH
Division of Vital Statistics
CERTIFICATE OF DEATH

State Office No. 117 2553

Register No. 164

1. PLACE OF DEATH

County Chippewa
Township Soo
Village
City Sault Ste. Marie — War Memorial Hospital (No. ___ St. ___ Ward)
(If death occurred in a hospital or institution, give its NAME instead of street and number)

2 FULL NAME Emily Fenlon
(a) Residence No. Hessel Michigan St., Ward ___
(Usual place of abode) (If non-resident give city or town and state)
Length of residence in city or town where death occurred ___ yrs. ___ mos. ___ ds. How long in U. S. if of foreign birth? ___ yrs. ___ mos. ___ da.

PERSONAL AND STATISTICAL PARTICULARS

3 SEX F.
4 Color or Race White
5 Single, Married, Widowed or Divorced (WRITE the word) Married

5a If married, widowed or divorced HUSBAND of (or) WIFE of Jos. P. Fenlon

6 DATE OF BIRTH (Month, day and year) May 7, 1871

7 AGE Years 63 Months 4 Days 28 If LESS than 1 day ___ hrs. OR ___ min.

OCCUPATION

8. Trade, profession, or particular kind of work done, as spinner, sawyer, bookkeeper, etc. Housewife

9. Industry or business in which work was done, as silk mill, saw mill, bank, etc. Home

10. Date deceased last worked at this occupation (month and year) Oct. 1

11. Total time (years) spent in this occupation ___

12. BIRTH PLACE (city or town) St. Ignace
(State or country) Michigan

FATHER

13. NAME John Hintz
14. BIRTHPLACE (city or town) Germany
(State or country)

MOTHER

15. MAIDEN NAME Emily Kroslien
16. BIRTHPLACE (city or town) Germany
(State or country)

17. INFORMANT Hintz J. Fenlon
(Address) Hessel Michigan

18. BURIAL, CREMATION, OR REMOVAL
Place Hessel Date Oct. 8, 1934

19. UNDERTAKER [illegible]
(Address) 1113 Maple St.

20. FILED 10-11 By [illegible] Cottrell
Registrar.

MEDICAL CERTIFICATE OF DEATH

21. DATE OF DEATH (month, day, and year) Oct 5, 1934

22. I HEREBY CERTIFY, That I attended deceased from 10-3--, 1934, to 10-5--, 1934
I last saw h__ alive on 10-5--, 1934 death is said to have occurred on the date stated above, at 9:40 P. m.
The principal cause of death and related causes of importance were as follows:

Organic Heart Disease   Duration ___

Other contributory causes of importance: ___

If operation, date of ___
Condition for which performed ___
Organ or part affected ___
Was there laboratory test? ___ Autopsy? ___
In case of violence state if accident, homicide or suicide ___
no
Where did injury occur? ___
(Specify city, county or state)
In industry, home or public place? ___
Was disease or injury related to occupation of deceased? ___
Signed G. R. Conrad M.D.
Address Sault Ste. Marie Mich.

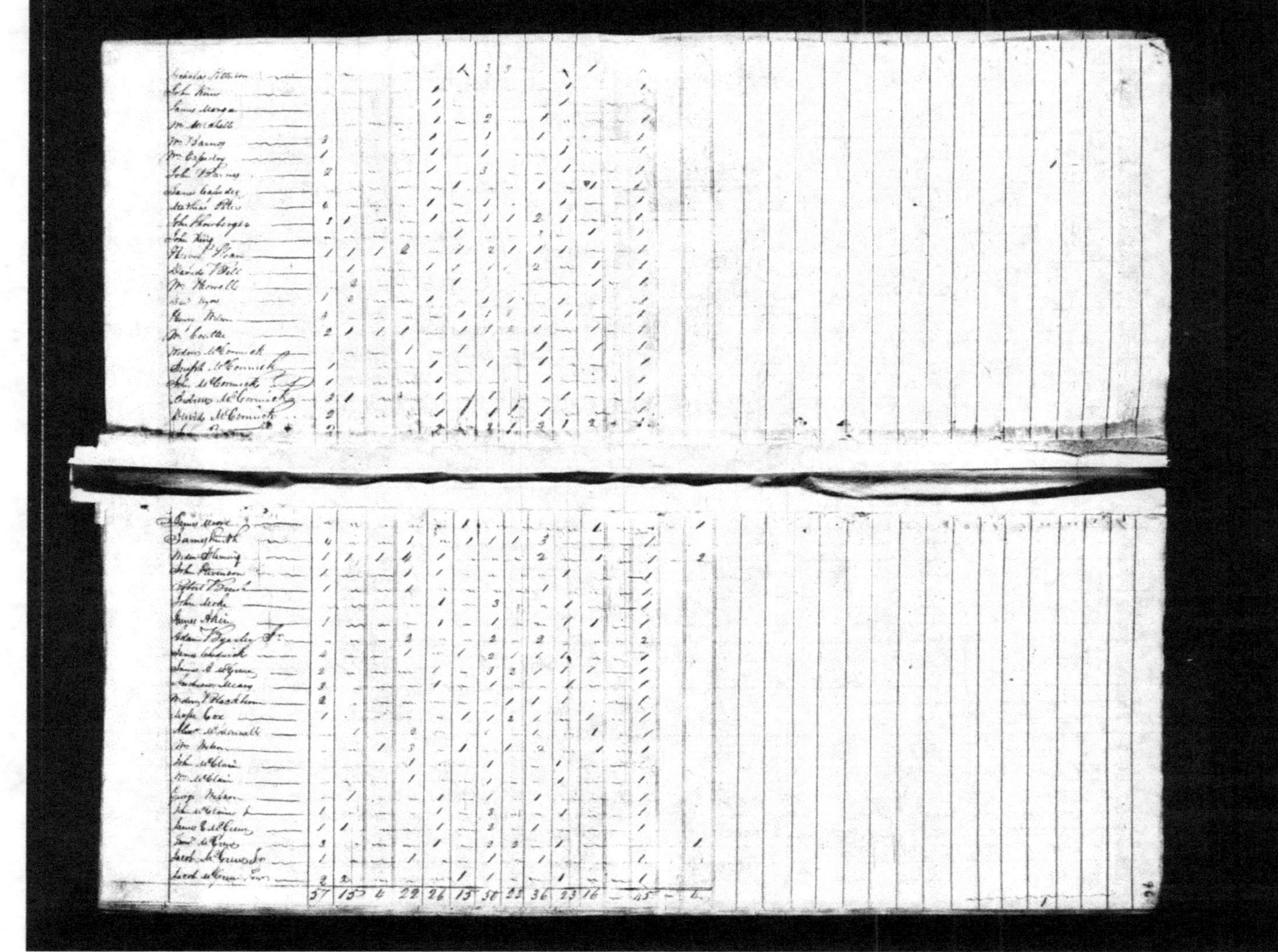

Upper leaf (household heads):

Nicholas Tillison
John Kline
James Morgan
Wm Mitchell
Wm Barnes
Wm Capasley
John Barnes
James Gatesley
Mathias Otter
John Hamberger
John King
Edward Sloan
David Gill
Wm Howell
Edwd Tyne
Henry Wilson
Wm Coulter
Widow McCormick
Joseph McCormick
John McCormick
Andrew McCormick
David McCormick

Lower leaf (household heads):

James Moore
James Smith
Moses Fleming
John Stevenson
Robert Brush
John Cook
James Akin
Adam Byerley Jr
James Chadwick
James McElgun
Andrew McCary
Wm Blackburn
Joseph Cox
Alexr McDonnell
Wm Nelson
John McClain
Wm McClain
George Nelson
John McClain Jr
James C McClean
Saml McRives
Jacob McGrew Sr
Jacob McGrew Jr

Column totals (bottom row): 57 | 15 | 6 | 29 | 26 | 15 | 58 | 25 | 36 | 23 | 16 | — | 45 | — | 6

DECLARATION OF INTENTION.

THE STATE OF OHIO, *Franklin County, ss.* } **PROBATE COURT.**

Personally Appeared in open Court *Edward Fenlow* an alien, who being duly sworn, deposes and says that he is a native of *Ireland* that he arrived in the United States in the month of *May* A. D. 1884, and it is bona fide his intention to become a Citizen of the United States of America, and to renounce forever, all allegiance and fidelity to any Foreign Prince, Potentate, State, or Sovereignty, and particularly to *Victoria Queen of Great Britain & Ireland* whose subject he is.

Edward + Fenlow
his mark

Sworn to before me, and signed in my presence, this *22* day of *June* A. D. 1885

Charles G. Saffen
Probate Judge and ex-officio Clerk.

THE STATE OF OHIO, *Franklin County, ss.* } **PROBATE COURT.**

BE IT REMEMBERED, That on the *22nd* day of *June* in the year of our Lord one thousand eight hundred and eighty *five* personally appeared before me *Charles G. Saffen* Judge and ex-officio Clerk of the Probate Court, within and for the County of Franklin, and State of Ohio, *Edward Fenton* an alien, a native of *Ireland* and makes report of himself for Naturalization; who being duly sworn according to law on his oath, doth declare and say it is bona fide his intention to become a Citizen of the United States of America, and to renounce forever, all allegiance and fidelity to any Foreign Prince, Potentate, State or Sovereignty, and particularly to *Victoria Queen of Great Britain and Ireland* whose subject he is.

ATTEST:

Charles G. Saffen
Probate Judge and ex-officio Clerk.

[This comprises all persons subject to do military duty between the ages of twenty and thirty-five years, and all unmarried persons subject to military duty above the age of thirty-five years and under the age of forty-five. Class II comprises all other persons subject to military duty.]

SCHEDULE II.—CONSOLIDATED LIST of all persons of CLASS II, subject to do military duty in the *Twenty first* Congressional District, consisting of the Counties of *Indiana Westmoreland* and *Fayette* State of *Pennsylvania*, enumerated during the month of *June*, 1863, under direction of *Capt Wm B Coulter*, Provost Marshal.

RESIDENCE		NAME	Age 1st July 1863	White or Colored.	Profession, Occupation, or Trade.	Place of Birth (Naming the State, Territory, or Country.)	Former Military Service	Remarks	
moreland									
...wick Bor	1 1	Light Elias	35	White	Hotelkeeper	Penna			1
...nsburg Bor	2 2	Lowery William C	38	"	Horsedealer	"			2
...fayette Tp	3 3	Leasure Lolan S?	36	"	Minister	"			3
"	4 4	Leasure John S	35	"	Justice Peace	"			4
"	5 5	Long Samuel	40	"	Stock Dealer	"			5
"	6 6	Long John	37	"	Shoemaker	"			6
"	7 7	Long Simon	44	"	Farmer	"			7
"	8 8	Long Jacob	35	"	Carpenter	"			8
"	9 9	Long Adam	40	"	Farmer	"			9
"	10 10	Long Andrew	36	"	"	"			10
"	11 11	Long Daniel	37	"	"	"			11
"	12 12	Lontz David	36	"	"	"			12
"	13 13	Latimer William	39	"	"	"			13
...ingdon Tp 14	14 14	Leightty Eli C	43	"	Brickmaker	"			14
"	15 15	Lans Bennett	42	"	Farmer				15
"	16 16	Lynn James S	57	"	"	"			16
"	17 17	Lopp Henry	43	"	Laborer	"			17
"	18 18	Lunchberger Frederick	43	"	Miner	Germany			18
"	19 19	Lutta Ephraim	40	"	Farmer	Penna			19
Sewickley	20 20	Lash Asa	42	"	"	"			20

A Muster Roll of the late Capt. Kinney's Company in the 4th Regiment of Jersey in the Service of the United States Commanded by Ephraim Martin Esqr. Taken for the Month of October 1778

Commission'd } Jany 6 — 1777 — Saml Conn Lieut

No	Serjeants	Enlisted	W	34	9m	Remarks
1	Dennis Hinds	✓	1			
2	Thomas Potter	✓	1			on Com[d] at Newark
3	Saml Powell	✓	1			Do Monmouth
1	Jacob Wolinger Drm	✓	1			
	Privates					
1	Timothy Conner	✓	0	1	—	
2	Joshua Pandler	✓	1			
3	John Gerald	✓	1			
4	Robert Proctor	✓	1			
5	Joshua Hackett	✓	1			
6	William Gaskill	✓	1			
7	Wm. Irwin	✓	1			
8	John Slater	✓	1			
9	Thomas Russell	✓	1			
10	Robt Woodsides	✓	1			
11	John Campbell	June 1	0		1	
12	James Everton	✓	1			
13	Fredk Miller	✓	1			
14	Saml Bowen	✓	1			
15	Thomas White	✓	1			
16	Zabulon Browne	✓	1			
17	Joshua Marion		1			
18	Joshua Crammer	✓	1			
19	Walter Lounsbury	✓	1			
20	Chas Stephens	✓	1			
21	Thomas Finn	✓	1			

No	Corporals	Enlisted	W	34	9m	Remarks
5	Jesse Edwards	✓	1			
22	Wm. Prince	June 6	0		1	
23	Adolph Chabant	✓	1			
24	Joseph Miller	✓	1			
25	Hugh Crealey	✓	1			on Guard
26	William Howell	✓	1			do
27	Bowen Watts	✓	1			do
28	Wm. Culley	✓	1			do
29	William McDade	✓	1			do
30	James Kinsey	✓	1			do
31	Neal O'Neal	✓	1			do
32	William Griffiths	✓	1			do
33	James Boyles	✓	1			do
34	Henry Cargan	✓	1			On Command
35	Thomas Watkins	✓	1			do
36	William Morgan	✓	1			do
37	Abr Stewart	✓	1			do
38	James Christy	✓	1			do Monmth
39	Henry Lennington	✓	1			Sick present
40	William Howell	✓	1			do
41	George Furny	✓	1			Waggoner

This day Muster'd Capt Kinney's Company as specified in the above Roll.
Novr 3 1778

A Dickey B.C.M.

MICHIGAN
DEPARTMENT OF STATE
LANSING
VITAL STATISTICS DIVISION.

CERTIFICATE AND RECORD OF DEATH.

[The Registrar should number each certificate received at once, in space below, beginning with "No. 1" for each year.]

376

Place of death:
County _Mackinac_
Township ——
Village ——
City _St. Ignace_

Location in City: _3_ Ward; No. _State_ St.

REGISTERED NO. _34_

Full Name _Emily Hirsh_

Date of Death: MONTH _Oct_ DAY _12_ YEAR 190_1_

Hospital, Institution or Transient ——
Late or home Residence ——
How long an Inmate or Resident ——
Sex _Female_ Color _White_

Single, married, widowed or divorced _widow_

If married, age at (first) marriage _22_ years.

Parent of _8_ children, of whom _3_ are living.

Age: YEARS _72_ MONTHS —— DAYS ——

Date of Birth: YEAR OF BIRTH _1829_ MONTH —— DAY ——

Occupation, if over 10 years of age _None_

Name of father _Mr. Cripleau_   Birthplace of father (State or country) _Germany_

Maiden name of mother _unknown_   Birthplace of mother (State or country) _Germany_

Birthplace (State or country) _Germany_

Date of burial or removal _Oct 15th 190 1_   Place of burial or removal _Gros Cap. Mich_

Signature of undertaker _Frank S Walker_   Address of undertaker _St Ignace_

Certificate of Reporter.

The personal and family particulars herein given relative to deceased are true to the best of my knowledge and belief.

(Signed) ____ X

(Address) ____ X

Medical Certificate of Cause of Death.

I hereby certify that I attended deceased from _Oct 2_ 190 1 to _Oct 12_ 190 1, that I last saw her alive on _Oct 11_ 190 1, that she died on _Oct 12_ 190 1, about _8_ o'clock _A_ M., and that to the best of my knowledge and belief the **CAUSE OF DEATH** was as hereunder written:

DURATION OF EACH CAUSE.

DISEASE CAUSING DEATH* _Disease consequent of old age_ _15_

Immediate cause of death ____

Contributory causes or complications, if any ____

Post-mortem ____

Place where DISEASE CAUSING DEATH was contracted, if other than place of death. ____

*In case of a **Violent Death**, state (1) mode of injury and whether accidental, suicidal or homicidal; (2) what was the nature of the injury and the immediate cause of death; (3) contributory causes or conditions, e. g., septicemia. Also whether operation was performed, etc.

In deaths from tuberculosis, cancer, etc., always specify what organ or part of the body was affected. In septicemia, give cause, especially if puerperal.

Witness my hand this _12_ day of _Oct_ 190 1.

Signature of physician, health officer or coroner ____ _J. Darling_ M. D.

(Address) ____ _St Ignace Mich._

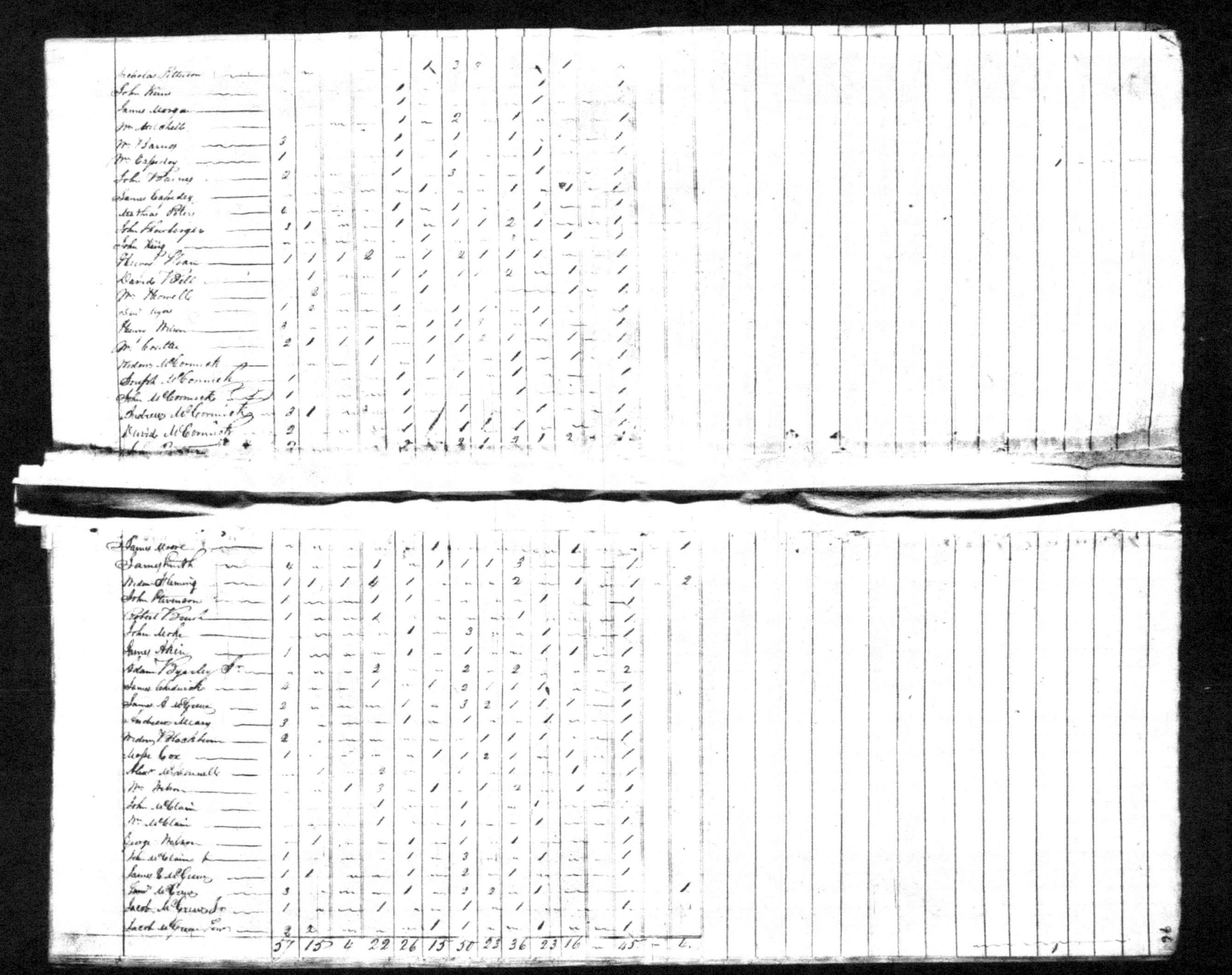

Nicholas Patterson
John Kinn
James Morgan
Wm Mitchell
Wm Barnes
Wm Cassaday
John Barnes
James Cassaday
Mathias Potter
John Shwoberger
John King
Thomas Sloan
David Bell
Wm Howell
Saml Lyon
Henry Wilson
Wm Coulter
Widow McCormick
Joseph McCormick
John McCormick
Andrew McCormick
David McCormick
James Moore
James Smith
William Fleming
John Stevenson
Robert Bousel
John Moke
James Akin
Adam Byerley Jr
James Chadwick
James S. McGrew
Andrew McCrary
Widow Blackburn
Moses Cox
Alex McDonnell
Wm Nelson
John McClain
Wm McClain
George Nelson
John McClain
James C. McGrew
Saml McGrew
Jacob McGrew Sr
Jacob McGrew Jr

Totals: 57 | 15 | 4 | 22 | 26 | 15 | 50 | 23 | 36 | 23 | 16 | — | 45 | — | L

No.	Name	Age		Sex/Status	Occupation	Origin	Destination
171	[illegible] Jensen	33		woman			
173	S. J. Möller	11		man	farmer		

Second Cabin & Nurses on Deck

No.	Name	Age		Sex/Status	Occupation	Origin	Destination
1	A. Thorson	22	b.	woman farmer			
2	Nels Torkelson	24	b.	man	do		
3	Nils Anderson	48	7.	man	do		
4	Anders Nilsson	17	10.	boy		Schweden	Illenvire
5	Elna Engelsson	53	6.	woman			
6	Anna Nilsson	22	—	woman			
7	Bengta Torkelson	16	6.	girl			
8	Anna Thorsson	8.	5.	girl			
9	Fried. Aug. Schreiber	14	9.	man	baker	Preussen	New York
10	Joh. Heiner. Wolff	34	6.	man	joiner	Holstein	Ohio
11	Pauline Levin	28.	8.	woman		Preussen	New York
12	Carl Jahl	30	7.	man	brewer	Preussen	Buffalo
13	Aug. F. Fr. W. Biedermann	22	6.	man	merchant clerk	Preussen	New York
14	Friedr. Kaspar	26	2.	man	chemist	Schleswig	New York
15	Samuel Salomon	38.	8.	man	farmer	Hamburg	Chicago
16	Friederike Salomon	—	9.	girl		Hamburg	Chicago
17	Johanna Salomon	26	6.	woman			
18	Joh. Fried. Pollhorn	26	7.	man	saddler		
19	Ernsthard El. Pollhorn	26	9.	girl		Preussen	Wisconsin
20	Joh. Dorotl. E. Pollhorn	23		girl			
21	Christline Fincker	25		girl		Preussen	Wisconsin
22	Christ. Friedr. Hiller	32.	5.	man		Preussen	Wisconsin
23	Albert Consul Spermann	30	9.	man	artist	Preussen	New York
24	Abraham Steil	21	7.	man	tailor	Oestreich	Ohio
25	Carl Heinr. Ferd. Johmann	26	16.	man	farmer	Preussen	Wisconsin
26	Aug. Carl S. Hans Wiemann	18	8.	man	farmer	Mecklenb. Schwerin	California
27	Heinr. Chr. Hennings	28	6.	man	merchant clerk	Mecklenb. Schwerin	Texas
28	Ernst Leder. Friedrich	24	3.	man	painter	Sachsen Altenburg	New York
29	J. Hans Foge	34	7.	man	farmer	Holstein	Iowa
30	Johann Kühl	26	9.	man	farmer	Holstein	Iowa
31	Carl Adolph Gebbers	38	—	man	gärtner	Preussen	Niagara
32	Georg Adolph v. Brandes	28	1.	man	goldsmith	Hannover	Mexico
33	Moritz Arons	17	6.	man	merchant clerk	Mecklenb. Schwerin	New York
34	Joh. Heinr. Joch. Heintze	34	6.	man	carpenter	Preussen	New York
35	Joh. Heinr. Fasel	22	6.	man	blacksmith	Mecklenb. Schwerin	Wisconsin
36	Adolph Alexander	23	2.	man	merchant	Preussen	New York
37	Hans H. Schmidt	49	5.	man	workman	Oldenburg	Iowa
38	Ilsa Margar. Schmidt	47	5.	woman		Holstein	Iowa
39	Claus Heinr. Fr. Schmidt	26	2.	man			
40	Joh. H. Christine Köhler	22	9.	woman		Sachsen Weimar	
41	Carl Reinhardt	32	—	man	blacksmith	Churhessen	
42	Auguste Reimschüssel	18		girl		Sachsen Weimar	New York
43	Schmidt Fänckel	53	5.	man	handwerker	New York	
44	Joh. Fr. Grabert	19		man	farmer	Mecklenb. Schwerin	

cab. 5   178

First Cabin

No.	Name	Age		Sex/Status	Occupation	Origin	Destination
1	Ernst Benjamin Stöcker	22	7.	man	bookseller	Preussen	Detroit
2	Joh. Chr. Becker	24	6.	man	chemist	Hamburg	Chicago
3	Carl Wilh. Alb. Eberhardt	24	2.	man	merchant clerk	Churhessen	Maryland
4	Fried. Wilh. Schreiber	21	6.	man	merchant clerk	Churhessen	Maryland
5	Anna Kennedy	21	6.	girl		New York	New York

222

Left Hamburg on the first day of May

S. H. Niemann

323

County _Mackinac_
Township ____
Village ____
City _St Ignace_

MICHIGAN
DEPARTMENT OF STATE—DIVISION OF VITAL STATISTICS.
CERTIFICATE AND RECORD OF DEATH

REGISTERED NO. _13_

Full name _John Hirtz_   Date of death   MONTH _May_   DAY _25_   YEAR 189_8_

Place of death _3_ Ward ____ St.   Sex _Male_   Color _W_

Single, married, widowed or divorced _Married_

If married, age at (first) marriage _30_ years.

Age   YEARS _76_   MONTHS ____   DAYS ____

Parent of _8_ children, of whom _3_ are living.   Birthplace (State or country) _Germany_

Occupation _Farmer_

Name of father _Claus Hirtz_   Birthplace of father (State or country) _German_

Maiden name of mother _Margaret Everett_   Birthplace of mother (State or country) _German_

Proposed date of burial or removal _May 28_ 189_8_

Proposed place of burial _Gro Cefo_

Proposed place of removal ____ via ____

Signature of undertaker _F S Walker_   Address of undertaker ____

Certificate of Reporter.

The personal and family particulars herein given relative to deceased are true to the best of my knowledge and belief. Witness my hand this ____ day of ____ 189___.

(Signature) ____

(Address) ____

Medical Certificate of Cause of Death.

I hereby certify that I attended deceased from _May 18_ 189_8_ to _May 26_ 189_8_ that I last saw h_ alive on _May 26_ 189_8_ that he died on _May 26_ 189_8_ about _10_ o'clock, _P_ M., and that to the best of my knowledge and belief the CAUSE OF DEATH was as hereunder written:

DURATION OF EACH CAUSE.

Disease causing death* _Cancer of Stomach_

Immediate cause of death ____

Contributory causes or complications, if any ____

Post mortem ____

*In case of a **Violent Death**, state (1) mode of injury and whether accidental, suicidal or homicidal; (2) what was the nature of the injury and the immediate cause of death; (3) contributory causes or conditions, e. g., septicemia. Also whether amputation was performed, etc.

Witness my hand this _27_ day of _May_ 189_8_

Signature of physician, health officer or coroner _W E Clark_ M. D.

(Address) _St Ignace Mich_

A Muster Roll of the late Capt. Kinney's Company in the 4th Regiment of Jersey in the Service of the United States Commanded by Gershom Martin Esqr. Taken for the Month of October 1778.

Commissioned} Jany 4 — 1777 — Saml. Conn Lieut.

No.	Serjeants	Enlisted	W	34	9m	Remarks
1	Dennis Hinds		1			
2	Thomas Potter		1			on Com. at Newark
3	Saml. Plivell		1			Do. Monmouth
1	Jacob Wolinger Dm		1			
	Privates					
1	Timothy Conner		0		1	—
2	Joshua Fandler		1			
3	John Gorald		1			
4	Robert Prooter		1			
5	Joshua Hackett		1			
6	William Gaskill		1			
7	Wm Irwin		1			
8	John Slater		1			
9	Thomas Bawell		1			
10	Robt Woodsides		1			
11	John Campbell	June 1	0		1	
12	James Emerton		1			
13	Fredk. Miller		1			
14	Saml. Bowen		1			
15	Thomas White		1			
16	Zabulon Browne		1			
17	Joshua Marrion		1			
18	Joshua Craumer		1			
19	Walter Lounsbury		1			
20	Chas Stephens		1			
21	Thomas Finn		1			

No.	Corporals	Enlisted	W	34	9m	Remarks
5	Jese Edwards		1			
22	Wm Prince	June 6	0		1	
23	Adolph Eubhart		1			
24	Joseph Miller		1			
25	Hugh Crawley		1			on Guard
26	William Howell		1			do
27	Bowen Watts		1			do
28	Wm Cubby		1			do
29	William McDade		1			do
30	James Kinney		1			do
31	Neal O'Neal		1			do
32	William Griffiths		1			do
33	James Boyles		1			do
34	Henry Cargan		1			On command
35	Thomas Watkins		1			do
36	William Morgan		1			do
37	Aber Stewart		1			do
38	James Christy		1			Wd. Monmo
39	Henry Lennington		1			Sick present
40	William Howell		1			do
41	George Farney		1			Waggoner

This day Muster'd Capt Kinney's Company as specified in the above Roll.

Novr. 3 1778

A. Dickey D.C.M.

Sergeant.

Grier, William.

Drummer.

Galley, Daniel, January 1, 1777.

Privates.

Gehen, Peter.
George, William, (e,) February 3, 1777.
Grady, David, became insane, and placed in Penn'a hospital by
  order of Col. Humpton, in 1779.
Gray, Joel.
Grimes, Philip, (e.)
Grosquill, John.

Corporals.

Harvey, George.
Horner, John.

Fifer.

Hainey, Henry.

Privates.

Hackett, Nicholas.
Harper, Thomas, (e,) resided in Pickens county, Alabama, 1834,
  aged seventy-six.
Hartman, Jacob, Douglass' company; wounded above the knee at
  Brandywine, and discharged in 1779; resided in Reading in
  1792.
Heaton, Edward.
Herrington, Jacob, resided in Crawford county, 1817.
Hill, Matthew.
Hostleberger, Philip.
Houghey, Patrick, transferred to Third Penn'a.
Howell, William, died in Westmoreland county, February 11, 1827,
  aged seventy-eight.

Sergeants.

John, Lewis, June, 1777; discharged November, 1778; unfit for
  service.
Johnston, Thomas, died in Dearborn county, Indiana, May 26,
  1823.

Private.

Jenkins, Israel, (e.)

Sergeants.

Kain, Matthew.
Kenny, Barnet.
Killan, James.